797,885 Books

are available to read at

Forgotten Books

www.ForgottenBooks.com

Forgotten Books' App
Available for mobile, tablet & eReader

ISBN 978-1-330-67949-4
PIBN 10091313

This book is a reproduction of an important historical work. Forgotten Books uses state-of-the-art technology to digitally reconstruct the work, preserving the original format whilst repairing imperfections present in the aged copy. In rare cases, an imperfection in the original, such as a blemish or missing page, may be replicated in our edition. We do, however, repair the vast majority of imperfections successfully; any imperfections that remain are intentionally left to preserve the state of such historical works.

Forgotten Books is a registered trademark of FB &c Ltd.
Copyright © 2015 FB &c Ltd.
FB &c Ltd, Dalton House, 60 Windsor Avenue, London, SW19 2RR.
Company number 08720141. Registered in England and Wales.

For support please visit www.forgottenbooks.com

1 MONTH OF FREE READING

at

www.ForgottenBooks.com

By purchasing this book you are eligible for one month membership to ForgottenBooks.com, giving you unlimited access to our entire collection of over 700,000 titles via our web site and mobile apps.

To claim your free month visit:
www.forgottenbooks.com/free91313

* Offer is valid for 45 days from date of purchase. Terms and conditions apply.

Similar Books Are Available from
www.forgottenbooks.com

Sacred Songs and Solos
Twelve Hundred Hymns, by Ira David Sankey

David
Shepherd, Psalmist, King, by F. B. Meyer

The Christian Hymnal
Hymns With Tunes for the Services of the Church, by Frank Sewell

A Complete Concordance to the Holy Scriptures
by John Eadie

Blossoms from a Believer's Garden
by Frances Ridley Havergal

A Book of Prayer
From the Public Ministrations of Henry Ward Beecher, by Henry Ward Beecher

The Chief Sufferings of Life, and Their Remedies
by Abbe Ephrem Duhaut

Companions of the Sorrowful Way
by John Watson

The Complete Works of Stephen Charnock, Vol. 1
by Stephen Charnock

Hymns from the Rigveda
Selected and Metrically Translated, by A. A. Macdonell

Counsel and Comfort for Daily Life
by Unknown Author

Hymn and Tune Book, for the Church and the Home
by American Unitarian Association

Meditations on the Sacred Passion of Our Lord
by Cardinal Wiseman

Devotions Upon Emergent Occasions
Together With Death's Duel, by John Donne

The Divine Processional
by Denis Wortman

Evening Thoughts
by Frances Ridley Havergal

The Every Day of Life
by James Russell Miller

Family Prayers
by Lyman P. Powell

Church Psalmist, or Psalms and Hymns
For the Public, Social, and Private Use of Evangelical Christians, by Free Will Baptists

Guide to Non-Liturgical Prayer
For Clergymen and Laymen, by John C. Clyde

The Prayers of
Doctor SAMUEL JOHNSON

Edited by   W. A. Bradley

New York
McClure, Phillips and Company
MCMII

Copyright MCMIII
By McClure, Phillips & Co.
Published November, MCMII, R.

Decorations by William Jordan

The publishers feel that some apology is
due the public for the lateness of this
book, which, scheduled for last November, only now makes its appearance in
February. Various obstacles have been
encountered in the course of the making, the most serious of which was
the bankruptcy of one printing
house at a crucial moment which
necessitated the transfer of all
plates and material from that
establishment to one in another city. It is hoped,
however, that the book
itself will compensate
for any annoyance
caused by the delay
in the case of
all who placed
their orders
in the au-
tumn.

Erratum.

Page 89, in the note on the portrait, at the top of the page, the word <u>recent</u> should be second.

I. Introductory.

O GOD who desirest not the death of a Sinner, look down with mercy upon me now daring to call upon thee. Let thy Holy Spirit so purify my affections, and exalt my desires that my prayer may be acceptable in thy sight, through Jesus Christ. Amen.

II. Prayers composed by Dr. Johnson on New Year's Day.

ALMIGHTY and everlasting God, in whose hands are life and death, by whose will all things were created, and by whose providence they are sustained, I return thee thanks that Thou hast given me life, and that thou hast continued it to this time, that thou hast hitherto forborne to snatch me away in the midst of Sin and Folly, and hast permitted me still to enjoy the means of Grace, and vouchsafed to call me yet again to Repentance. Grant, O merciful Lord, that thy Call may not be vain, that my Life may not be continued to encrease my Guilt, and that thy gracious Forbearance may not harden my heart in wickedness. Let me remember, O my God, that as Days and Years pass over me, I approach nearer to the Grave, where there is no repentance, and grant, that by the assistance of thy Holy Spirit, I may so pass through this Life, that I may obtain Life everlasting, for the Sake of our Lord Jesus Christ. Amen.

II

ALMIGHTY and most merciful Father, who has not yet suffered me to fall into the Grave, grant that I may so remember my past Life, as to repent of the days and years which I have spent in forgetfulness of thy mercy, and neglect of my own Salvation, and so use the time which thou shalt yet allow me, as that I may become every day more diligent in the duties which in thy Providence shall be assigned me, and that when at last I shall be called to judgment I may be received as a good and faithful servant into everlasting happiness, for the sake of Jesus Christ our Lord. Amen.

III

ALMIGHTY God, by whose will I was created, and by whose Providence I have been sustained, by whose mercy I have been called to the knowledge of my Redeemer, and by whose Grace whatever I have thought or acted acceptable to thee has been inspired and directed, grant, O Lord, that in reviewing my past life, I may recollect thy mercies to my preservation, in whatever state thou preparest for me, that in affliction I may remember how often I have been succoured, and in Prosperity may know and confess from whose hand the blessing is received.

Let me, O Lord, so remember my sins, that I may abolish them by true repentance, and so improve the Year to which thou hast graciously extended my life, and all the years which thou shalt yet allow me, that I may hourly become purer in thy sight; so that I may live in thy fear, and die in thy favour, and find mercy at the last day, for the sake of Jesus Christ. Amen.

IV

ALMIGHTY God, who hast continued my life to this day, grant that, by the assistance of thy Holy Spirit, I may improve the time which thou shalt grant me, to my eternal salvation. Make me to remember, to thy glory, thy judgments and thy mercies. Make me so to consider the loss of my wife, whom thou hast taken from me, that it may dispose me, by thy grace, to lead the residue of my life in thy fear. Grant this, O Lord, for Jesus Christ's sake. Amen.

V

ALMIGHTY and everlasting God, in whom we live and move, and have our being, glory be to thee, for my recovery from sickness, and the continuance of my life. Grant O my God that I may improve the year which I am now beginning, and all the days which thou shalt add to my life, by serious repentance and diligent obedience, that, by the help of thy holy Spirit I may use the means of Grace to my own salvation, and at last enjoy thy presence in eternal happiness, for Jesus Christ's sake.   Amen.

VI

ALMIGHTY God, who hast brought me to the beginning of another year, and by prolonging my life invitest to repentance, forgive me that I have mispent the time past, enable me from this instant to amend my life according to thy holy Word, grant me thy Holy Spirit, that I may so pass through things temporal as not finally to lose the things eternal.   O God, hear my prayer for the sake of Jesus Christ.   Amen.

VII

ALMIGHTY and most merciful Father, I again appear in thy presence the wretched mispender of another year which thy mercy has allowed me.   O Lord let me not sink into total depravity, look down upon me, and rescue me at last from the captivity of Sin. Impart to me good resolutions, and give me strength and perseverance to perform them. Take not from me thy Holy Spirit, but grant that I may redeem the time lost, and that by temperance and diligence, by sincere repentance and faithful Obedience I may finally obtain everlasting happiness, for the sake of Jesus Christ our Lord. Amen.

VIII

ALMIGHTY and most merciful Father, in whose hands are life and death, as thou hast suffered me to see the beginning of another year, grant, I beseech thee, that another year may not be lost in Idleness, or squandered in unprofitable employment. Let not sin prevail on the remaining part of life, and take not from me thy Holy Spirit, but as every day brings me nearer to my end, let every day contribute to make my end holy and happy. Enable me O Lord, to use all enjoyments with due temperance, preserve me from unseasonable and immoderate sleep, and enable me to run with diligence the race that is set before me, that, after the troubles of this life, I may obtain everlasting happiness, through Jesus Christ our Lord. Amen.

IX

ALMIGHTY and most merciful Father, who hast continued my life from year to year, grant that by longer life I may become less desirous of sinful pleasures, and more careful of eternal happiness. As age comes upon me let my mind be more withdrawn from vanity and folly, more enlightened with the knowledge of thy will, and more invigorated with resolution to obey it. O Lord, calm my thoughts, direct my desires, and fortify my purposes. If it shall please thee give quiet to my latter days, and so support me with thy grace that I may dye in thy favour for the sake of Jesus Christ our Lord. Amen.

X

ALMIGHTY God by whose mercy I am permitted to behold the beginning of another year, succour with thy help and bless with thy favour, the creature whom Thou vouchsafest to preserve. Mitigate, if it shall seem best unto thee, the diseases of my body, and compose the disorders of my mind. Dispel my terrours; and grant that the time which thou shalt yet allow me, may not pass unprofitably away. Let not pleasure seduce me, Idleness lull me, or misery depress me. Let me perform to thy glory, and the good of my fellow creatures the work which thou shalt yet appoint me. And grant that as I draw nearer to my dissolution, I may, by the help of thy Holy Spirit feel my knowledge of Thee encreased, my hope exalted, and my Faith strengthened, that, when the hour which is coming shall come, I may pass by a holy death to everlasting happiness, for the sake of Jesus Christ our Lord. Amen.

XI

ALMIGHTY God, who hast permitted me to see the beginning of another year, enable me so to receive thy mercy, as that it may raise in me stronger desires of pleasing thee by purity of mind and holiness of Life. Strengthen me, O Lord, in good purposes, and reasonable meditations. Look with pity upon all my disorders of mind, and infirmities of body. Grant that the residue of my life may enjoy such degrees of health as may permit me to be useful, and that I may live to thy Glory; and O merciful Lord when it shall please thee to call me from the present state, enable me to dye in confidence of thy mercy, and receive me to everlasting happiness, for the sake of Jesus Christ our Lord. Amen.

XII

ALMIGHTY God, by whose mercy my life has been yet prolonged to another year, grant that thy mercy may not be in vain. Let not my years be multiplied to encrease my guilt, but as age advances, let me become more pure in my thoughts, more regular in my desires, and more obedient to thy laws. Let not the cares of the world distract me, nor the evils of age overwhelm me. But continue and encrease thy loving kindness towards me, and when thou shalt call me hence, receive me to everlasting happiness, for the sake of Jesus Christ, our Lord.   Amen.

XIII

ALMIGHTY God, merciful Father, who hatest nothing that thou hast made, but wouldest that all should be saved, have mercy upon me. As thou hast extended my Life, encrease my strength, direct my purposes, and confirm my resolution, that I may truly serve Thee, and perform the duties which Thou shalt allot me. ¶ Relieve, O gracious Lord, according to thy mercy the pains and distempers of my Body, and appease the tumults of my Mind. Let my Faith and Obedience encrease as my life advances, and let the approach of Death incite my desire to please Thee, and invigorate my diligence in good works, till at last, when Thou shalt call me to another state, I shall lie down in humble hope, supported by thy Holy Spirit, and be received to everlasting happiness, through Jesus Christ our Lord. Amen.

XIV

ALMIGHTY God, merciful Father, who hast permitted me to see the beginning of another year, grant that the time which thou shalt yet afford me may be spent to thy glory, and the salvation of my own Soul. Strengthen all good resolutions. Take not from me thy Holy Spirit, but have mercy upon me, and shed thy Blessing both on my soul and body, for the sake of Jesus Christ our Lord. Amen.

XV

ALMIGHTY Lord, merciful Father vouchsafe to accept the thanks which I now presume to offer thee for the prolongation of my life. Grant, O Lord, that as my days are multiplied, my good resolutions may be strengthened, my power of resisting temptations encreased, and my struggles with snares and obstructions invigorated. Relieve the infirmities both of my mind and body. Grant me such strength as my duties may require and such diligence as may improve those opportunities of good that shall be offered me. Deliver me from the intrusion of evil thoughts. Grant me true repentance of my past life, and as I draw nearer and nearer to the grave, strengthen my Faith, enliven my Hope, extend my Charity, and purify my desires, and so help me by thy Holy Spirit that when it shall be thy pleasure to call me hence, I may be received to everlasting happiness, for the sake of thy Son Jesus Christ our Lord. Amen.

XVI

ALMIGHTY God, merciful Father, who hast granted to me the beginning of another year, grant that I may employ thy gifts to thy glory, and my own salvation. Excite me to amend my life. Give me good resolutions, and enable me to perform them. As I approach the Grave let my Faith be invigorated, my Hope exalted, and my Charity enlarged. Take not from me thy Holy Spirit, but in the course of my life protect me, in the hour of death sustain me, and finally receive me to everlasting happiness, for the sake of Jesus Christ. Amen.

XVII

ALMIGHTY God, my Creator and Preserver by whose mercy my life has been continued to the beginning of another year, grant me with encrease of days, encrease of Holiness, that as I live longer, I may be better prepared to appear before thee, when thou shalt call me from my present state. ¶ Make me, O Lord, truly thankful for the mercy which Thou hast vouchsafed to shew me through my whole life; make me thankful for the health which thou hast restored in the last year, and let the remains of my strength and life be employed to thy glory and my own salvation. ¶ Take not, O Lord, Thy holy Spirit from me; enable me to avoid or overcome all that may hinder my advancement in Godliness; let me be no longer idle, no longer sinful; but give me rectitude of thought and constancy of action, and bring me at last to everlasting happiness for the sake of Jesus Christ, our Lord and Saviour. Amen.

XVIII

ALMIGHTY God merciful Father, who hast granted me such continuance of Life, that I now see the beginning of another year, look with mercy upon me, as thou grantest encrease of years, grant encrease of Grace. Let me live to repent what I have done amiss, and by thy help so to regulate my future life, that I may obtain mercy when I appear before thee, through the merits of Jesus Christ. Enable me, O Lord, to do my duty with a quiet mind; and take not from me thy Holy Spirit, but protect and bless me, for the sake of Jesus Christ. Amen.

III. Prayers Composed by Dr. Johnson on Easter Day.

O LORD, who givest the grace of Repentance, and hearest the prayers of the penitent, grant, that by true contrition, I may obtain forgiveness of all the sins committed, and of all duties neglected, in my union with the Wife whom thou hast taken from me, for the neglect of joint devotion, patient exhortation, and mild instruction. And, O Lord, who canst change evil to good, grant that the loss of my Wife may so mortify all inordinate affections in me, that I may henceforth please thee by holiness of Life. ⁋ And, O Lord, so far as it may be lawful for me, I commend to thy fatherly goodness the Soul of my departed wife; beseeching thee to grant her whatever is best in her present state, and finally to receive her to eternal happiness. And this I beg for Jesus Christ's sake, whose death I am now about to commemorate. To whom &c. Amen.

II

ALMIGHTY God, heavenly Father, who desirest not the death of a sinner, look down with mercy upon me depraved with vain imaginations, and entangled in long habits of sin. Grant me that grace without which I can neither will nor do what is acceptable to thee. Pardon my sins, remove the impediments that hinder my obedience. Enable me to shake off sloth, and to redeem the time mispent in idleness and sin by a diligent application of the days yet remaining to the duties which thy Providence shall allot me. O God, grant me thy Holy Spirit that I may repent and amend my life, grant me contrition, grant me resolution for the sake of Jesus Christ, to whose covenant I now implore admission, of the benefits of whose death I implore participation. For his sake have mercy on me, O God; for his sake, O God, pardon and receive me. Amen.

III

ALMIGHTY and most merciful Father, who hast created me to love and to serve thee, enable (me) so to partake of the sacrament in which the Death of Jesus Christ is commemorated that I may henceforward lead a new life in thy faith and fear. Thou who knowest my frailties and infirmities strengthen and support me. Grant me thy Holy Spirit, that after all my lapses I may now continue stedfast in obedience, that after long habits of negligence and sin, I may, at last, work out my salvation with diligence and constancy, purify my thoughts from pollutions, and fix my affections on things eternal. Much of my time past has been lost in sloth, let not what remains, O Lord, be given me in vain, but let me from this time lead a better life and serve thee with a quiet mind through Jesus Christ our Lord.   Amen.

IV

ALMIGHTY and most merciful Father, look down with pity upon my sins. I am a sinner, good Lord; but let not my sins burthen me for ever. Give me thy grace to break the chain of evil custom. Enable me to shake off idleness and sloth; to will and to do what thou hast commanded; grant me chaste in thoughts, words and actions; to love and frequent thy worship, to study and understand thy word; to be diligent in my calling, that I may support myself and relieve others. ⁋ Forgive me, O Lord, whatever my mother has suffered by my fault, whatever I have done amiss, and whatever duty I have neglected. Let me not sink into useless dejection; but so sanctify my affliction, O Lord, that I may be converted and healed; and that, by the help of thy holy spirit, I may obtain everlasting life through Jesus Christ our Lord. ⁋ And, O Lord, so far as it may be lawful, I commend unto thy fatherly goodness my father, brother, wife, and mother, beseeching thee to make them happy for Jesus Christ's sake.   Amen.

V

ALMIGHTY and most merciful Father look down upon my misery with pity, strengthen me that I may overcome all sinful habits, grant that I may with effectual faith commemorate the death of thy Son Jesus Christ, so that all corrupt desires may be extinguished, and all vain thoughts may be dispelled. Enlighten me with true knowledge, animate me with reasonable hope, comfort me with a just sense of thy love, and assist me to the performance of all holy purposes, that after the sins, errours, and miseries of this world, I may obtain everlasting happiness for Jesus Christ's sake. To whom &c. Amen.

VI

ALMIGHTY and most merciful Father, who by thy son Jesus Christ hast redeemed man from Sin and Death, grant that the commemoration of his passion may quicken my repentance, encrease my hope, and strengthen my faith and enlarge my Charity; that I may lament and forsake my sins and for the time which thou shalt yet grant me, may avoid Idleness, and neglect of thy word and worship. Grant me strength to be diligent in the lawful employments which shall be set before me; Grant me purity of thoughts, words, and actions. Grant me to love and study thy word, and to frequent thy worship with pure affection. Deliver and preserve me from vain terrours, and grant that by the Grace of thy Holy Spirit I may so live that after this life ended, I may be received to everlasting happiness for the sake of Jesus Christ our Lord. Amen.

VII

ALMIGHTY and most merciful Father, who hast created and preserved me, have pity on my weakness and corruption. Deliver me from habitual wickedness and idleness, enable me to purify my thoughts, to use the faculties which Thou hast given me with honest diligence, and to regulate my life by thy holy word. Grant me, O Lord, good purposes and steady resolution, that I may repent my sins, and amend my life. Deliver me from the distresses of vain terrour, and enable me by thy Grace to will and to do what may please thee, that when I shall be called away from this present state I may obtain everlasting happiness through Jesus Christ our Lord. Amen.

VIII

ALMIGHTY and most merciful Father, who hatest nothing that thou hast made, nor desirest the Death of a Sinner, look down with mercy upon me, and grant that I may turn from my wickedness and live. Forgive the days and years which I have passed in folly, idleness, and sin. Fill me with such sorrow for the time mispent, that I may amend my life according to thy holy word; Strengthen me against habitual idleness, and enable me to direct my thoughts to the performance of every duty; that while I live I may serve thee in the state to which thou shalt call me, and at last by a holy and happy death be delivered from the struggles and sorrows of this life, and obtain eternal happiness by thy mercy, for the sake of Jesus Christ our Lord. Amen.

IX

ALMIGHTY and most merciful Father! before whom I now appear laden with the sins of another year, suffer me yet again to call upon Thee for pardon and peace. ¶ O God! grant me repentance, grant me reformation. Grant that I may be no longer distracted with doubts and harassed with vain terrors. Grant that I may no longer linger in perplexity, nor waste in idleness that life which Thou hast given and preserved. Grant that I may serve Thee in firm faith and diligent endeavour, and that I may discharge the duties of my calling with tranquility and constancy. Take not, O God, Thy holy Spirit from me: but grant that I may so direct my life by Thy holy laws, as that, when Thou shalt call me hence, I may pass by a holy and happy death to a life of everlasting and unchangeable joy, for the sake of Jesus Christ our Lord.   Amen.

X

ALMIGHTY and everlasting God, who hast preserved me by thy fatherly care through all the years of my past Life, and now permittest me again to commemorate the sufferings and the merits of our Lord and Saviour Jesus Christ grant me so to partake of this holy Rite, that the disquiet of my mind may be appeased, that my Faith may be encreased, my hope strengthened, and my Life regulated by thy Will.   Make me truly thankful for that portion of health which thy mercy has restored, and enable me to use the remains of Life to thy glory and my own salvation.   Take not from me O Lord thy Holy Spirit.   Extinguish in my mind all sinful and inordinate desires.   Let me resolve to do that which is right, and let me by thy help keep my resolutions.   Let me, if it be best for me, at last know peace and comfort, but whatever state of life Thou shalt appoint me let me end it by a happy death, and enjoy eternal happiness in thy presence, for the sake of Jesus Christ our Lord.   Amen.

XI

ALMIGHTY and most merciful Father, I am now about to commemorate once more in thy presence, the redemption of the world by our Lord and Saviour thy Son Jesus Christ. Grant, O most merciful God, that the benefit of his sufferings may be extended to me. Grant me Faith, grant me Repentance. Illuminate me with thy Holy Spirit. Enable me to form good purposes, and to bring these purposes to good effect. Let me so dispose my time, that I may discharge the duties to which thou shalt vouchsafe to call me, and let that degree of health, to which thy mercy has restored me be employed to thy Glory. O God, invigorate my understanding, compose my pertubations, recal my wanderings, and calm my thoughts, that having lived while thou shalt grant me life, to do good and to praise Thee, I may when thy call shall summon me to another state, receive mercy from thee, for Jesus Christ's sake. Amen.

XII

ALMIGHTY God, merciful Father, who hatest nothing that thou hast made, look down with pity on my sinfulness and weakness. Strengthen, O Lord, my mind, deliver me from needless terrours. Enable me to correct all inordinate desires, to eject all evil thoughts, to reform all sinful habits, and so to amend my life, that when at the end of my days thou shalt call me hence, I may depart in peace, and be received into everlasting happiness, for the sake of Jesus Christ our Lord. Amen.

XIII

GLORY be to Thee, O Lord God, for the deliverance which Thou hast granted me from diseases of mind and body. Grant, O gracious God, that I may employ the powers which Thou vouchsafest me to thy Glory, and the Salvation of my soul, for the sake of Jesus Christ. Amen.

XIV

ALMIGHTY God, by whose mercy I am now about to commemorate the death of my Redeemer, grant that from this time I may so live as that his death may be efficacious to my eternal happiness. Enable me to conquer all evil customs. Deliver me from evil and vexatious thoughts. Grant me light to discover my duty, and Grace to perform it. As my life advances, let me become more pure, and more holy. Take not from me thy Holy Spirit, but grant that I may serve thee with diligence and confidence; and when thou shalt call me hence, receive me to everlasting happiness, for the sake of Jesus Christ our Lord. Amen.

XV

ALMIGHTY God, heavenly Father, whose mercy is over all thy works, look with pity on my miseries and sins. Suffer me to commemorate in thy presence my redemption by thy Son Jesus Christ. Enable me so to repent of my mispent time that I may pass the residue of my life in thy fear and to thy glory. Relieve, O Lord, as seemeth best unto thee, the infirmities of my body, and the pertubations of my mind. Fill my thoughts with awful love of thy Goodness, with just fear of thine Anger, and with humble confidence in thy Mercy. Let me study thy laws, and labour in the duties which thou shalt set before me. Take not from me thy Holy Spirit, but incite in me such good desires as may produce diligent endeavours after thy Glory and my own salvation; and when, after hopes and fears, and joys and sorrows thou shalt call me hence, receive me to eternal happiness, for the Sake of Jesus Christ our Lord. Amen.

XVI

ALMIGHTY and most merciful Father, who hast preserved me by thy tender forbearance, once more to commemorate thy Love in the Redemption of the world, grant that I may so live the residue of my days, as to obtain thy mercy when thou shalt call me from the present state. Illuminate my thoughts with knowledge, and inflame my heart with holy desires. Grant me to resolve well, and keep my resolutions. Take not from me thy Holy Spirit, but in life and in death have mercy on me for Jesus Christs sake.   Amen.

XVII

ALMIGHTY and most merciful Father, who seest all our miseries, and knowest all our necessities, Look down upon me and pity me. Defend me from the violent incursions of evil thoughts, and enable me to form and keep such resolutions as may conduce to the discharge of the duties which thy Providence shall appoint me, and so help me by thy Holy Spirit, that my heart may surely there be fixed where true joys are to be found, and that I may serve Thee with pure affection and a cheerful mind. Have mercy upon me, O God, have mercy upon me; years and infirmities oppress me, terrour and anxiety beset me   Have mercy upon me, my Creatour and my Judge. In all dangers protect me, in all perplexities relieve and free me, and so help me by thy Holy Spirit, that I may now so commemorate the death of thy Son our Saviour Jesus Christ as that when this short and painful life shall have an end, I may for his sake be received to everlasting happiness.   Amen.

XVIII

ALMIGHTY and most merciful Father, suffer me once more to commemorate the death of thy Son Jesus Christ, my Saviour and Redeemer, and make the memorial of his death profitable to my salvation, by strengthening my Faith in his merits, and quickening my obedience to his laws. Remove from me, O God, all inordinate desires, all corrupt passions, & all vain terrours; and fill me with zeal for thy glory, and with confidence in thy mercy. Make me to love all men, and enable me to use thy gifts, whatever thou shalt bestow, to the benefit of my fellow creatures. So lighten the weight of years, and so mitigate the afflictions of disease that I may continue fit for thy service, and useful in my station. And so let me pass through this life by the guidance of thy Holy Spirit, that at last I may enter into eternal joy, through Jesus Christ our Lord. Amen.

XIX

ALMIGHTY God, by thy merciful continuance of my life, I come once more to commemorate the sufferings and death of thy Son

Jesus Christ, and to implore that mercy which for his sake thou shewest to sinners. Forgive me my sins, O Lord, and enable me to forsake them. Ease, if it shall please thee, the anxieties of my mind, and relieve the infirmities of my Body. Let me not be disturbed by unnecessary terrours, and let not the weakness of age make me unable to amend my life. O Lord, take not from me thy Holy Spirit, but receive my petitions, succour and comfort me, and let me so pass the remainder of my days, that when thou shalt call me hence I may enter into eternal happiness through Jesus Christ our Lord. Amen.

XX

ALMIGHTY God, merciful Father, by whose Protection I have been preserved, and by whose clemency I have been spared, grant that the life which thou hast so long continued, may be no longer wasted in idleness or corrupted by wickedness. Let my future purposes be good, and let not my good purposes be vain. Free me O Lord from vain terrours, and strengthen me in diligent obedience to thy laws. Take not from me thy Holy Spirit, but enable me so to commemorate the death of my Saviour Jesus Christ, that I may be made partaker of his merits, and may finally, for his sake obtain everlasting happiness. Amen.

XXI

ALMIGHTY God, my Creator and my Judge, who givest life and takest it away, enable me to return sincere and humble thanks for my late deliverance from imminent death. So govern my future life by the Holy Spirit, that every day which thou shalt permit to pass over me, may be spent in thy service, and leave me less tainted with wickedness, and more submissive to thy will. ¶ Enable me, O Lord, to glorify thee for that knowledge of my Corruption, and that sense of thy wrath, which my desease and weakness, and danger awakened in my mind. Give me such sorrow as may purify my heart, such indignation as may quench all confidence in myself, and such repentance as may by the intercession of my Redeemer obtain pardon. Let the commemoration of the sufferings and Death of thy Son which I am now, by thy favour, once more permitted to make, fill me with faith, hope, and charity. Let my purposes be good and my resolutions unshaken, and let me not be hindred or distracted by vain and useless fears, but through the time which yet remains guide me by thy Holy Spirit, and finally receive me to everlasting life, for the sake of Jesus Christ our Lord and Saviour. Amen.

IV. Prayers composed by Dr. Johnson in memory of his wife.

ALMIGHTY and most merciful Father, who lovest those whom Thou punishest, and turnest away thy anger from the penitent, look down with pity upon my sorrows, and grant that the affliction which it has pleased Thee to bring upon me, may awaken my conscience, enforce my resolutions of a better life, and impress upon me such conviction of thy power and goodness, that I may place in Thee my only felicity, and endeavour to please Thee in all my thoughts, words, and actions. Grant, O Lord, that I may not languish in fruitless and unavailing sorrow, but that I may consider from whose hand all good and evil is received, and may remember that I am punished for my sins, and hope for comfort only by repentance. Grant, O merciful God, that by the assistance of thy Holy Spirit I may repent, and be comforted, obtain that peace which the world cannot give, pass the residue of my life in humble resignation and cheerful obedience; and when it shall please Thee to call me from this mortal state, resign myself into thy hands with faith and confidence, and finally obtain mercy and everlasting happiness, for the sake of Jesus Christ our Lord. Amen.

II

O LORD, our heavenly Father, almighty and most merciful God, in whose hands are life and death, who givest and takest away, castest down and raisest up, look with mercy on the affliction of thy unworthy servant, turn away thine anger from me, and speak peace to my troubled soul. Grant me the assistance and comfort of thy Holy Spirit, that I may remember with thankfulness the blessings so long enjoyed by me in the society of my departed wife; make me so to think on her precepts and example, that I may imitate whatever was in her life acceptable in thy sight, and avoid all by which she offended Thee. Forgive me, O merciful Lord, all my sins, and enable me to begin and perfect that reformation which I promised her, and to persevere in that resolution, which she implored Thee to continue, in the purposes which I recorded in thy sight, when she lay dead before me, in obedience to thy laws, and faith in thy word. And now, O Lord, release me from my sorrow, fill me with just hopes, true faith, and holy consolations, and enable me to do my duty in that state of life to which thou hast been pleased to call me, without disturbance from fruitless grief, or tumultuous imaginations; that in all my thoughts, words, and actions, I may glorify thy Holy Name, and finally obtain, what I hope Thou hast granted to thy departed servant, everlasting joy and felicity, through our Lord Jesus Christ. Amen.

III

O LORD! Governour of heaven and earth, in whose hands are embodied and departed Spirits, if thou hast ordained the Souls of the Dead to minister to the Living, and appointed my departed Wife to have care of me, grant that I may enjoy the good effects of her attention and ministration, whether exercised by appearance, impulses, dreams or in any other manner agreeable to thy Government. Forgive my presumption, enlighten my ignorance, and however meaner agents are employed, grant me the blessed influences of thy holy Spirit, through Jesus Christ our Lord. Amen.

IV

O LORD, our heavenly Father, without whom all purposes are frustrate, all efforts are vain, grant me the assistance of thy Holy Spirit, that I may not sorrow as one without hope, but may now return to the duties of my present state with humble confidence in thy protection, and so govern my thoughts and actions, that neither business may withdraw my mind from Thee, nor idleness lay me open to vain imaginations; that neither praise may fill me with pride, nor censure with discontent; but that in the changes of this life, I may fix my heart upon the reward which Thou hast promised to them that serve Thee, and that whatever things are true, whatever things are honest, whatever things are just, whatever are pure, whatever are lovely, whatever are of good report, wherein there is virtue, wherein there is praise, I may think upon and do, and obtain mercy and everlasting happiness. Grant this, O Lord, for the sake of Jesus Christ. Amen.

V

O GOD, who on this day wert pleased to take from me my dear Wife, sanctify to me my sorrows and reflections. Grant, that I may renew and practise the resolutions which I made when thy afflicting hand was upon me. Let the remembrance of thy judgments by which my wife is taken away awaken me to repentance, and the sense of thy mercy by which I am spared, strengthen my hope and confidence in Thee, that by the assistance and comfort of thy holy spirit I may so pass through things temporal, as finally to gain everlasting happiness, and to pass by a holy and happy death, into the joy which thou hast prepared for those that love thee. Grant this, O Lord, for the sake of Jesus Christ. Amen.

VI

ALMIGHTY God, vouchsafe to sanctify unto me the reflections and resolutions of this day, let not my sorrow be unprofitable; let not my resolutions be vain. Grant that my grief may produce true repentance, so that I may live to please thee, and when the time shall come that I must die like her whom thou hast taken from me, grant me eternal happiness in thy presence, through Jesus Christ our Lord. Amen.

VII

ALMIGHTY God, our heavenly father whose judgments terminate in mercy grant, I beseech Thee, that the remembrance of my Wife, whom Thou hast taken from me, may not load my soul with unprofitable sorrow, but may excite in me true repentance of my sins and negligences, and by the operation of thy Grace may produce in me a new life pleasing to thee. Grant that the loss of my Wife may teach me the true use of the Blessings which are yet left me; and that, however bereft of worldly comforts, I may find peace and refuge in thy service through Jesus Christ our Lord. Amen.

VIII

ALMIGHTY and eternal God, who givest life and takest it away, grant that while thou shalt prolong my continuance on earth, I may live with a due sense of thy mercy and forbearance, and let the remembrance of her whom thy hand has separated from me, teach me to consider the shortness and uncertainty of life, and to use all diligence to obtain eternal happiness in thy presence. O God enable me to avoid sloth, and to attend heedfully and constantly to thy word and worship. Whatever was good in the example of my departed wife, teach me to follow; and whatever was amiss give me grace to shun, that my affliction may be sanctified, and that remembering how much every day brings me nearer to the grave, I may every day purify my mind, and amend my life, by the assistance of thy holy Spirit, till at last I shall be accepted by Thee, for Jesus Christ's sake. Amen.

IX

O GOD, Giver and Preserver of all life, by whose power I was created, and by whose providence I am sustained, look down upon me (with) tenderness and mercy, grant that I may not have been created to be finally destroyed, that I may not be preserved to add wickedness to wickedness, but may so repent me of my sins, and so order my life to come, that when I shall be called hence like the wife whom Thou hast taken from me, I may dye in peace and in thy favour, and be received into thine everlasting kingdom through the merits and mediation of Jesus Christ thine only Son our Lord and Saviour. Amen.

V. Prayers composed by Dr. Johnson on his birthday.

OGOD, the Creatour and Preserver of all Mankind, Father of all mercies, I thine unworthy servant do give Thee most humble thanks, for all thy goodness and lovingkindness to me. I bless Thee for my Creation, Preservation, and Redemption, for the knowledge of thy Son Jesus Christ, for the means of Grace and the Hope of Glory. In the days of Childhood and Youth, in the midst of weakness, blindness and danger, Thou hast protected me; amidst Afflictions of Mind, Body and Estate, Thou hast supported me; and amidst vanity and Wickedness Thou hast spared me. Grant, O merciful Father, that I may have a lively sense of thy mercies. Create in me a contrite Heart, that I may worthily lament my sins and acknowledge my wickedness, and obtain Remission and forgiveness, through the satisfaction of Jesus Christ. And, O Lord, enable me, by thy Grace, to redeem the time which I have spent in Sloth, Vanity, and wickedness; to make use of thy Gifts to the honour of thy Name; to lead a new life in thy Faith, Fear, and Love; and finally to obtain everlasting Life. Grant this, Almighty Lord, for the merits and through the mediation of our most holy and blessed Saviour Jesus Christ; to whom, with Thee and the Holy Ghost, Three Persons and one God, be all honour and Glory, world without end. Amen.

II

ALMIGHTY and most merciful Father by whose providence my life has been prolonged, and who hast granted me now to begin another year of probation, vouchsafe me such assistance of thy Holy Spirit, that the continuance of my life may not add to the measure of my guilt, but that I may so repent of the days and years passed in neglect of the duties which thou hast set before me, in vain thoughts, in sloth, and in folly, that I may apply my heart to true wisdom, by diligence redeem the time lost, and by repentance obtain pardon for the sake of Jesus Christ. Amen.

III

ALMIGHTY and most merciful Father, who yet sparest and yet supportest me, who supportest me in my weakness, and sparest me in my sins, and hast now granted me to begin another year, enable me to improve the time which is yet before me, to thy glory and my own Salvation. Impress upon my Soul such repentance of the days mispent in idleness and folly, that I may henceforward diligently attend to the business of my station in this world, and to all the duties which thou hast commanded. Let thy Holy Spirit comfort and guide me that in my passage through the pains or pleasures of the present state, I may never be tempted to forgetfulness of Thee. Let my life be useful, and my death be happy; let me live according to thy laws, and dye with just confidence in thy mercy for the sake of Jesus Christ our Lord. Amen.

IV

O ALMIGHTY God, merciful Father, who hast continued my life to another year grant that I may spend the time which thou shalt yet give me in such obedience to thy word and will that finally, I may obtain everlasting life. Grant that I may repent and forsake my sins before the miseries of age fall upon me, and that while my strength yet remains I may use it to thy glory and my own salvation, by the assistance of thy Holy Spirit, for Jesus Christ's sake. Amen.

V

O GOD, heavenly Father, who desirest not the death of a Sinner, grant that I may turn from my Wickedness and live. Enable me to shake off all impediments of lawful action, and so to order my life, that increase of days may produce increase of grace, of tranquillity of thought, and vigour in duty. Grant that my resolves may be effectual to a holy life, and a happy death, for Jesus Christs sake. Amen.

VI

ALMIGHTY and most merciful Father, who hast granted me to prolong my life to another year, look down upon me with pity. Let not my manifold sins and negligences avert from me thy fatherly regard. Enlighten my mind that I may know my duty, that I may perform it, strengthen my resolution. Let not another year be lost in vain deliberations; let me remember, that of the short life of man, a great part is already past, in sinfulness and sloth. Deliver me, gracious Lord, from the bondage of evil customs, and take not from me thy Holy Spirit; but enable me so to spend my remaining days, that, by performing thy will I may promote thy glory, and grant that after the troubles and disappointments of this mortal state I may obtain everlasting happiness for the sake of Jesus Christ our Lord. Amen.

VII

ALMIGHTY and most merciful Father, Creator and Preserver of mankind, look down with pity upon my troubles and maladies. Heal my body, strengthen my mind, compose my distraction, calm my inquietude, and relieve my terrours, that if it please thee, I may run the race that is set before me with peace patience constancy and confidence. Grant this O Lord, and take not from me thy Holy Spirit, but pardon and bless me for the sake of Jesus Christ our Lord. Amen.

VIII

ALMIGHTY and most merciful Father, I now appear in thy presence, laden with the sins, and accountable for the mercies of another year. Glory be to thee, O God, for the mitigation of my troubles, and for the hope of health both of mind and body which thou hast vouchsafed me. Most merciful Lord, if it seem good unto thee, compose my mind, and relieve my diseases; enable me to per form the duties of my station, and so to serve thee, as that, when my hour of departure from this painful life shall be delayed no longer, I may be received to everlasting happiness, for the sake of Jesus Christ our Lord. Amen.

IX

ALMIGHTY and everlasting God, whose mercy is over all thy works, and who hast no pleasure in the Death of a Sinner, look with pity upon me, succour and preserve me; enable me to conquer evil habits, and surmount temptations. Give me Grace so to use the degree of health which Thou hast restored to my Mind and Body, that I may perform the task thou shalt yet appoint me. Look down, O gracious Lord upon my remaining part of Life; grant, if it please thee, that the days few or many which thou shalt yet allow me, may pass in reasonable confidence, and holy tranquillity. Withhold not thy Holy Spirit from me, but strengthen all good purposes till they shall produce a life pleasing to Thee. And when thou shalt call me to another state, forgive me my sins, and receive me to Happiness, for the Sake of Jesus Christ our Lord. Amen.

X

ALMIGHTY God, most merciful Father, look down upon me with pity; Thou hast protected me in childhood and youth, support me, Lord in my declining years. Preserve me from the dangers of sinful presumption. Give me, if it be best for me, stability of purposes, and tranquillity of mind. Let the year which I have now begun, be spent to thy glory, and to the furtherance of my salvation. Take not from me thy holy Spirit, but as Death approaches, prepare me to appear joyfully in thy presence for the sake of Jesus Christ our Lord. Amen.

XI

O GOD by whom all things were created and are sustained, who givest and takest away, in whose hands are life and death, accept my imperfect thanks for the length of days which thou hast vouchsafed to grant me, impress upon my mind such repentance of the time mispent in sinfulness and negligence, that I may obtain forgiveness of all my offences, and so calm my mind and strengthen my resolutions that I may live the remaining part of my life in thy fear, and with thy favour. Take not thy Holy Spirit from me, but let me so love thy laws, and so obey them, that I may finally be received to eternal happiness, through Jesus Christ our Lord. Amen.

XII

ALMIGHTY and most merciful Father, who hast brought me to the beginning of another year, grant me so to remember thy gifts, and so to acknowledge thy goodness, as that every year and day which thou shalt yet grant me, may be employed in the amendment of my life, and in the diligent discharge of such duties, as thy Providence shall allot me. Grant me, by thy Grace, to know and to do what Thou requirest. Give me good desires, and remove those impediments which may hinder them from effect. Forgive me my sins, negligences, and ignorances, and when at last thou shalt call me to another life, receive me to everlasting happiness, for the sake of Jesus Christ our Lord. Amen.

XIII

ALMIGHTY God, Creator of all things in whose hands are Life and death, glory be to thee for thy mercies, and for the prolongation of my Life to the common age of Man. Pardon me, O gracious God, all the offences which in the course of seventy years I have committed against thy holy laws, and all negligences of those Duties which thou hast required. Look with pity upon me, take not from me thy Holy Spirit, but enable me to pass the days which thou shalt yet vouchsafe to grant me, in thy Fear and to thy Glory; and accept O Lord, the remains of a mispent life, that when Thou shalt call me to another state, I may be received to everlasting happiness for the sake of Jesus Christ our Lord. Amen.

XIV

ALMIGHTY God, my Creator and Preserver, who hast permitted me to begin another year, look with mercy upon my wretchedness and frailty. Rectify my thoughts, relieve my perplexities, strengthen my purposes, and reform my doings. Let encrease of years bring encrease of Faith, Hope, and Charity. Grant me diligence in whatever work thy Providence shall appoint me. Take not from me thy Holy Spirit but let me pass the remainder of the days which thou shalt yet allow me, in thy fear and to thy Glory; and when it shall be thy good pleasure to call me hence, grant me, O Lord, forgiveness of my sins, and receive me to everlasting happiness, for the sake of Jesus Christ our Lord. Amen.

XV

ALMIGHTY and most merciful Father, who hast added another year to my life, and yet permittest me to call upon thee, Grant that the remaining days which thou shalt yet allow me may be past in thy fear and to thy glory, grant me good resolutions and steady perseverance. Relieve the diseases of my body and compose the disquiet of my mind. Let me at last repent and amend my life, and, O Lord, take not from me thy Holy Spirit, but assist my amendment, and accept my repentance, for the sake of Jesus Christ.   Amen.

XVI

ALMIGHTY God, merciful Father, who art the giver of all good enable me to return Thee due thanks for the continuance of my life and for the great mercies of the last year, for relief from the diseases that afflicted me, and all the comforts and alleviations by which they were mitigated; and O my gracious God make me truly thankful for the call by which thou hast awakened my conscience, and summoned me to Repentance. Let not thy call, O Lord, be forgotten or thy summons neglected, but let the residue of my life, whatever it shall be, be passed in true contrition, and diligent obedience. Let me repent of the sins of my past years and so keep thy laws for the time to come, that when it shall be thy good pleasure to call me to another state, I may find mercy in thy sight.   Let thy Holy Spirit support me in the hour of death, and O Lord grant me pardon in the day of Judgment, for the sake of Jesus Christ, our Lord.   Amen.

VI. Prayers composed by Dr. Johnson on several occasions.

ALMIGHTY God, the giver of all good things, without whose help all Labour is ineffectual, and without whose grace all wisdom is folly, grant, I beseech Thee, that in this my undertaking, thy Holy Spirit may not be withheld from me, but that I may promote thy glory, and the Salvation both of myself and others; grant this, O Lord, for the sake of Jesus Christ. Amen.

II

ALMIGHTY God, in whose hands are all the powers of man; who givest understanding, and takest it away; who, as it seemeth good unto Thee, enlightenest the thoughts of the simple, and darkenest the meditations of the wise, be present with me in my studies and enquiries. ⁋ Grant, O Lord, that I may not lavish away the life which Thou hast given me on useless trifles, nor waste it in vain searches after things which Thou hast hidden from me. ⁋ Enable me, by thy Holy Spirit, so to shun sloth and negligence, that every day may discharge part of the task which Thou hast allotted me; and so further with thy help that labour which, without thy help, must be ineffectual, that I may obtain, in all my undertakings, such success as will most promote thy glory, and the salvation of my own soul, for the sake of Jesus Christ. Amen.

III

O LORD, in whose hands are life and death, by whose power I am sustained, and by whose mercy I am spared, look down upon me with pity. Forgive me, that I have this day neglected the duty which Thou hast assigned to it, and suffered the hours, of which I must give account, to pass away without any endeavour to accomplish thy will, or to promote my own salvation. Make me to remember, O God, that every day is thy gift, and ought to be used according to thy command. Grant me, therefore, so to repent of my negligence, that I may obtain mercy from Thee, and pass the time which Thou shalt yet allow me, in diligent performance of thy commands, through Jesus Christ. Amen.

IV

O GOD, who hast hitherto supported me, enable me to proceed in this labour, and in the whole task of my present state; that when I shall render up, at the last day, an account of the talent committed to me, I may receive pardon, for the sake of Jesus Christ. Amen.

V

O LORD, who hast ordained labour to be the lot of man, and seest the necessities of all thy creatures, bless my studies and endeavours; feed me with food convenient for me; and if it shall be thy good pleasure to intrust me with plenty, give me a compassionate heart, that I may be ready to relieve the wants of others; let neither poverty nor riches estrange my heart from Thee, but assist me with thy grace so to live as that I may die in thy favour, for the sake of Jesus Christ. Amen.

VI

O LORD God, almighty disposer of all things, in whose hands are life and death, who givest comforts and takest them away, I return Thee thanks for the good example of Hill Boothby, whom Thou hast now taken away, and implore thy grace, that I may improve the opportunity of instruction which Thou hast afforded me, by the knowledge of her life, and by the sense of her death; that I may consider the uncertainty of my present state, and apply myself earnestly to the duties which Thou hast set before me, that living in thy fear, I may die in thy favour, through Jesus Christ our Lord. Amen.

VII

ALMIGHTY God, who hast restored light to my eye, and enabled me to persue again the studies which Thou hast set before me; teach me, by the diminution of my sight, to remember that whatever I possess is thy gift, and by its recovery, to hope for thy mercy: and, O Lord, take not thy Holy Spirit from me; but grant that I may use thy bounties according to thy will, through Jesus Christ our Lord. Amen.

VIII

ALMIGHTY God, merciful Father, in whose hands are life and death, sanctify unto me the sorrow which I now feel. Forgive me whatever I have done unkindly to my Mother, and whatever I have omitted to do kindly. Make me to remember her good precepts, and good example, and to reform my life according to thy holy word, that I may lose no more opportunities of good; I am sorrowful, O Lord, let not my sorrow be without fruit. Let it be followed by holy resolutions, and lasting amendment, that when I shall die like my mother, I may be received to everlasting life. ¶ I commend, O Lord, so far as it may be lawful, into thy hands, the soul of my departed Mother, beseeching Thee to grant her whatever is most beneficial to Her in her present state. ¶ O Lord, grant me thy Holy Spirit, and have mercy upon me for Jesus Christ's sake.   Amen.

IX

ALMIGHTY God, heavenly Father, who hast graciously prolonged my life to this time, and by the change of outward things which I am now to make, callest me to a change of inward affections, and to a reformation of my thoughts, words and practices.   Vouchsafe merciful Lord that this call may not be vain.   Forgive me whatever has been amiss in the state which I am now leaving, Idleness, and neglect of thy word and worship.   Grant me the grace of thy Holy Spirit, that the course which I am now beginning may proceed according to thy laws, and end in the enjoyment of thy favour.   Give me, O Lord, pardon and peace, that I may serve thee with humble confidence, and after this life enjoy thy presence in eternal Happiness. ¶ And, O Lord, so far as it may be lawful for me, I commend to thy Fatherly goodness, my Father, my Brother, my Wife, my Mother.   I beseech thee to look mercifully upon them, and grant them whatever may most promote their present and eternal joy. ¶ O Lord, hear my prayers for Jesus Christs sake, to whom, with Thee and the Holy

Ghost three persons and one God be all honour and glory world without end.   Amen.

X

ALMIGHTY God, the Giver of wisdom, without whose help resolutions are vain, without whose blessing study is ineffectual, enable me, if it be thy will, to attain such knowledge as may qualify me to direct the doubtful, and instruct the ignorant, to prevent wrongs, and terminate contentions; and grant that I may use that knowledge which I shall attain, to thy glory, and my own salvation, for Jesus Christ's sake.   Amen.

XI

ALMIGHTY God, who art the Giver of all Wisdom, enlighten my understanding with knowledge of right, and govern my will by thy laws, that no deceit may mislead me, nor temptation corrupt me, that I may always endeavor to do good, and to hinder evil. Amidst all the hopes and fears of this world, take not thy Holy Spirit from me, but grant that my thoughts may be fixed on thee, and that I may finally attain everlasting happiness, for Jesus Christs sake.   Amen.

XII

ALMIGHTY and most merciful Father, who hast graciously supplied me with new conveniences for study, grant that I may use thy gifts to thy glory. Forgive me the time mispent, relieve my perplexities, strengthen my resolution, and enable me to do my duty with vigour and constancy; and when the fears and hopes, the pains and pleasures of this life shall have an end, receive me to everlasting happiness, for the sake of Jesus Christ our Lord. Amen.

XIII

O GOD, grant that I may practise such temperance in Meat, Drink and Sleep, and all bodily enjoyments, as may fit me for the duties to which thou shalt call me, and by thy blessing procure my freedom of thought and quietness of mind, that I may so serve Thee in this short and frail life, that I may be received by Thee at my death to everlasting happiness. Take not O Lord thy Holy Spirit from me, deliver me not up to vain fears, but have mercy on me, for the sake of Jesus Christ our Lord. Amen.

XIV

ALMIGHTY and most merciful Father, whose loving-kindness is over all thy works, behold, visit, and relieve this thy Servant, who is grieved with sickness. Grant that the sense of her weakness may add strength to her faith, and seriousness to her Repentance. And grant that by the help of thy Holy Spirit after the pains and labours of this short life, we may all obtain everlasting happiness through Jesus Christ our Lord, for whose sake hear our prayers. Amen.

XV

ALMIGHTY God, who seest that I have no power of myself to help myself; keep me both outwardly in my body, and inwardly in my soul, that I may be defended from all adversities that may happen to the body, and from all evil thoughts which may assault and hurt the soul, through Jesus Christ our Lord. Amen.

XVI

O LORD, who wouldst that all men should be saved, and who knowest that without thy grace we can do nothing acceptable to thee, have mercy upon me, enable me to break the chain of my sins, to reject sensuality in thought, and to overcome and suppress vain scruples;

and to use such diligence in lawful employment as may enable me to support myself and do good to others. O Lord, forgive me the time lost in idleness; pardon the sins which I have committed, and grant that I may redeem the time misspent, and be reconciled to thee by true repentance, that I may live and die in peace, and be received to everlasting happiness. Take not from me, O Lord, thy Holy Spirit, but let me have support and comfort for Jesus Christ's sake. Amen.

XVII

ALMIGHTY God, giver of all knowledge, enable me so to pursue the study of tongues, that I may promote thy glory and my own salvation. ⁌ Bless my endeavours, as shall seem best unto Thee; and if it shall please Thee to grant me the attainment of my purpose, preserve me from sinful pride; take not thy Holy Spirit from me, but give me a pure heart and humble mind, through Jesus Christ. Amen.

XVIII

ALMIGHTY God, merciful Father, whose providence is over all thy works, look down with pity upon the diseases of my body, and the perturbations of my mind. Give thy Blessing, O Lord, to the means which I shall use for my relief, and restore ease to my body, and quiet to my thoughts. Let not my remaining life be made useless by infirmities, neither let health, if thou shalt grant it, be employed by me in disobedience to thy laws; but give me such a sense of my pains, as may humble me before thee; and such remembrance of thy mercy as may produce honest industry, and holy confidence. And, O Lord, whether Thou ordainest my days to be past in ease or anguish, take not from me thy Holy Spirit; but grant that I may attain everlasting life, for the sake of Jesus Christ our Lord. Amen.

XIX

O God who hast ordained that whatever is to be desired, should be sought by labour, and who by thy Blessing, bringest honest labour to good effect; look with mercy upon my studies and endeavours. Grant me, O Lord, to design only what is lawful and right, and afford me calmness of mind, and steadiness of purpose, that I may so do thy will in this short life, as to obtain happiness in the world to come, for the sake of Jesus Christ our Lord. Amen.

XX

ALMIGHTY God, our Creatour and Preserver, from whom proceedeth all good, enable me to receive with humble acknowledgment of thy unbounded benignity, and with due consciousness of my own unworthiness, that recovery and continuance of health which thou hast granted me, and vouchsafe to accept the thanks which I now offer. Glory be to Thee, O Lord, for this and all thy mercies. Grant, I beseech Thee, that the health and life which thou shalt yet allow me, may conduce to my eternal happiness. Take not from me thy Holy Spirit, but so help and bless me, that when Thou shalt call me hence I may obtain pardon and salvation, for the sake of Jesus Christ our Lord. Amen.

XXI

ALMIGHTY God who art the Giver of all good enable me to remember with due thankfulness the comforts and advantages which I have enjoyed by the friendship of Henry Thrale, for whom, so far as is lawful, I humbly implore thy mercy in his present state. O Lord, since thou hast been pleased to call him from this world, look with mercy on those whom he has left, continue to succour me by such means as are best for me, and repay to his relations the kindness which I have received from him; protect them in this world from temptations and calamities, and grant them happiness in the world to come, for Jesus Christs sake. Amen.

XXII

ALMIGHTY God, by whose mercy I am now permitted to commemorate my Redemption by our Lord Jesus Christ; grant that this aweful remembrance may strengthen my Faith, enliven my Hope, and increase my Charity; that I may trust in Thee with my whole heart, and do good according to my power. Grant me the help of thy Holy Spirit, that I may do thy will with diligence, and suffer it with humble patience; so that when Thou shalt call me to Judgment, I may obtain forgiveness and acceptance for the sake of Jesus Christ, our Lord and Saviour. Amen.

XXIII

GRANT, I beseech Thee, merciful Lord, that the designs of a new and better life, which by thy Grace I have now formed, may not pass away without effect. Incite and enable me by thy Holy Spirit, to improve the time which Thou shalt grant me; to avoid all evil thoughts words and actions; and to do all the duties which thou shalt set before me. Hear my prayer, O Lord, for the sake of Jesus Christ. Amen.

XXIV

ALMIGHTY God, Father of all mercy, help me by thy Grace that I may with humble and sincere thankfulness remember the comforts and conveniences which I have enjoyed at this place, and that I may resign them with holy submission, equally trusting in thy protection when Thou givest and when Thou takest away. Have mercy upon me, O Lord, have mercy upon me. ⁋ To thy fatherly protection, O Lord, I commend this family. Bless, guide, and defend them, that they may so pass through this world as finally to enjoy in thy presence everlasting happiness, for Jesus Christs sake. Amen.

XXV

ALMIGHTY God, Creator and Governor of the World, who sendest sickness and restorest health, enable me to consider, with a just sense of thy mercy, the deliverance which Thou hast lately granted me, and assist by thy Blessing, as is best for me, the means which I shall use for the cure of the disease with which I am now afflicted. Encrease my patience, teach me submission to thy will, and so rule my thoughts and direct my actions, that I may be finally received to everlasting happiness through Jesus Christ our Lord. Amen.

XXVI

ALMIGHTY God, who in thy late visitation hast shewn mercy to me, and now sendest to my companion disease and decay, grant me grace so to employ the life which thou hast prolonged, and the faculties which thou hast preserved, and so to receive the admonition which the sickness of my friend, by thy appointment, gives me, that I may be constant in all holy duties, and be received at last to eternal happiness. ¶ Permit, O Lord, thy unworthy creature to offer up this prayer for Anna Williams now languishing upon her bed, and about to recommend herself to thy infinite mercy. O God, who desirest not the death of a sinner, look down with mercy upon her: forgive her sins and strengthen her faith. Be merciful, O Father of Mercy, to her and to me: guide us by thy holy spirit through the remaining part of life; support us in the hour of death, and pardon us in the day of judgment, for Jesus Christ's sake. Amen.

XXVII

ALMIGHTY and most merciful Father, who art the Lord of life and death, who givest and takest away, teach me to adore thy providence, whatever Thou shalt allot me; make me to remember, with due thankfulness, the comforts which I have received from my friendship with Anna Williams. Look upon her, O Lord, with mercy, and prepare me, by thy grace, to die with hope, and to pass by death to eternal happiness, through Jesus Christ our Lord. Amen.

XXVIII

O God, most merciful Father who by many diseases hast admonished me of my approach to the end of life, and by this gracious addition to my days hast given me an opportunity of appearing once more in thy presence to commemorate the sacrifice by which thy son Jesus Christ has taken away the sins of the world, assist me in this commemoration by thy Holy Spirit that I may look back upon the sinfulness of my life past with pious sorrow, and efficacious Repentance, that my resolutions of amendment may be rightly formed and diligently exerted, that I may be freed from vain and useless scruples, and that I may serve thee with Faith, Hope, and Charity for the time which Thou shalt yet allow me, and finally be received to Everlasting Happiness for the sake of Jesus Christ, our Lord. Amen.

XXIX

O LORD, my Maker and Protector, who hast graciously sent me into this world, to work out my salvation, enable me to drive from me all such unquiet and perplexing thoughts as may mislead or hinder me in the practice of those duties which thou hast required. When I behold the works of thy hands and consider the course of thy providence, give me Grace always to remember that thy thoughts are not my thoughts, nor thy ways my ways. And while it shall please Thee to continue me in this world where much is to be done and little to be known, teach me by thy Holy Spirit to withdraw my mind from unprofitable and dangerous enquiries, from difficulties vainly curious, and doubts impossible to be solved. Let me rejoice in the light which thou hast imparted, let me serve thee with active zeal, and humble confidence, and wait with patient expectation for the time in which the soul which Thou receivest, shall be satisfied with knowledge. Grant this, O Lord, for Jesus Christ's sake. Amen.

XXX

ALMIGHTY and most merciful Father, who afflictest not willingly the children of Men, and by whose holy will... now languishes in sickness and pain, make, I beseech (Thee,) this punishment effectual to those gracious purposes for which thou sendest it, let it, if I may presume to ask, end not in death, but in repentance, let him live to promote thy kingdom on earth by the useful example of a better life, but if thy will be to call him hence, let his thoughts be so purified by his sufferings, that he may be admitted to eternal Happiness. And, O Lord, by praying for him, let me be admonished to consider my own sins, and my own danger, to remember the shortness of life, and to use the time which thy mercy grants me to thy glory and my own salvation, for the sake of Jesus Christ our Lord. Amen.

XXXI

ALMIGHTY God, our heavenly Father, without whose help labour is useless, without whose light search is vain, invigorate my studies and direct my enquiries, that I may, by due diligence and right discernment establish myself and others in thy holy Faith. Take not, O Lord, thy Holy Spirit from me, let not evil thoughts have dominion in my mind. Let me not linger in ignorance, but enlighten and support me, for the sake of Jesus Christ our Lord. Amen.

XXXII

O LORD God, in whose hands are the wills and affections of men, kindle in my mind holy desires, and repress sinful and corrupt imaginations; enable me to love thy commandments, and to desire thy promises; let me, by thy protection and influence, so pass through things temporal, as finally not to lose the things eternal; and among the hopes and fears, the pleasures and sorrows, the dangers and deliverances, and all the changes of this life, let my heart be surely fixed, by the help of thy Holy Spirit, on the everlasting fruition of thy presence, where true joys are to be found. Grant, O Lord, these petitions. Forgive, O merciful Lord, whatever I have done contrary to thy laws. Give me such a sense of my wickedness as may produce true contrition and effectual repentance, so that when I shall be called into another state, I may be received among the sinners to whom sorrow and reformation have obtained pardon, for Jesus Christ's sake. Amen.

XXXIII

ALMIGHTY and most merciful Father, whose clemency I now presume to implore, after a long life of carelessness and wickedness, have mercy upon me. I have committed many trespasses; I have neglected many duties. I have done what Thou hast forbidden, and left undone what Thou hast commanded. Forgive, merciful Lord, my sins, negligences, and ignorances, and enable me, by thy Holy Spirit, to amend my life according to thy Holy Word, for Jesus Christ's sake. Amen.

XXXIV

O MERCIFUL God, full of compassion, long-suffering, and of great pity, who sparest when we deserve punishment, and in thy wrath thinkest upon mercy; make me earnestly to repent, and heartily to be sorry for all my misdoings; make the remembrance so burdensome and painful, that I may flee to Thee with a troubled spirit and a contrite heart; and, O merciful Lord, visit, comfort, and relieve me; cast me not out from thy presence, and take not thy Holy Spirit from me, but excite in me true repentance; give me in this world knowledge of thy truth, and confidence in thy mercy, and in the world to come life everlasting, for the sake of our Lord and Saviour, thy Son Jesus Christ. Amen.

XXXV

ALMIGHTY and most merciful Father, I am now, as to human eyes it seems, about to commemorate, for the last time, the death of thy Son Jesus Christ our Saviour and Redeemer. Grant, O Lord, that my whole hope and confidence may be in his merits, and thy mercy; enforce and accept my imperfect repentance; make this commemoration available to the confirmation of my faith, the establishment of my hope, and the enlargement of my charity; and make the death of thy Son Jesus Christ effectual to my redemption. Have mercy upon me, and pardon the multitude of my offences. Bless my friends; have mercy upon all men. Support me, by the grace of thy Holy Spirit, in the days of weakness, and at the hour of death; and receive me, at my death, to everlasting happiness, for the sake of Jesus Christ. Amen.

REST ETERNAL, GRANT TO HIM, O LORD: AND LET LIGHT PERPETUAL SHINE UPON HIM. AMEN.

NOTES

AN INTRODUCTORY NOTE

IN 1785, the year after Johnson's death, the Reverend George Strahan, D. D., Prebendary of Rochester and Vicar of Islington in Middlesex, a man close to Johnson in later life, published a posthumous volume of writings by his friend to which he gave the title of Prayers and Meditations. In reality the book contained not only such matter as the title would seem strictly to indicate, but a most intimate record, in form approximating a journal or diary, though irregularly kept, of the spiritual experiences of Johnson's inner life. It revealed the man as few even among his friends had known him and it presents even to us who have long been in possession of the revelation, a strange contrast with our general conception of the character of Samuel Johnson. This conception we base upon Boswell's graphic picture of the man, colossal in figure and intellect, who exerted so confidently the sway of the born dictator of opinion over his associates in club and coffee-house or over the tavern board. We think of him as the moralist, man of the world and sententious yet witty apothegmatist who reduced the wisdom of living to practical maxims of common sense with the readiness and assurance of one for whom life held no hidden places of uncertainty and doubt. We therefore come a little unexpectedly in the Prayers and Meditations upon a phase of spiritual dependence unlooked for in one who strikes us mainly in all his intercourse with men by his intellectual ruggedness and moral self-reliance.

One side is perhaps necessary as a complement to the other. No one could live without relaxing, at intervals, in the tense moods of certainty that characterized Johnson as he appeared in public. And the man who is competent to lay down the law as the advocate of society and civilization and established doctrine for all men, must by the nature of his position be more often and more acutely aware than another of the inadequacy of these things and their inability to touch and sustain the spirit. On the other hand part of Johnson's positiveness in debate came as a reaction of relief in regaining the ground with which he was familiar after having groped his way through the tortuous paths of self-examination and the malarial lowlands of melancholy and private grief. But above and beyond this natural alternation of moods of intellectual tensity and relaxation, there was an actual and fundamental duality in Johnson's nature, the two notes of which, intellectual vigor and spiritual sensitiveness in which religious devotion was but a single element, existed side by side and separate each from the other.

This duality in Johnson is not without its larger significance for the age in which he lived. It affords an indication of that breaking up of the age's ideals, evidences of which were not then wanting in other fields, as for example, Methodism in religion and sentimentalism in poetry, which was to lead the century to romanticism at its close. On one side of his work Johnson expressed as no other had done with equal force and completeness the practical common sense wisdom of eighteenth century philosophy. On the other he expresses, privately and tentatively to be sure, the tendency of his age to abandon this philosophy and to fall back upon a more personal and direct sense of existence and responsibility. And on this side the Prayers and Meditations take rank with the Confessions of Rousseau as a manifesto of the new order.

The circumstances through which the records of Johnson's inner, spiritual life came into the hands of their editor and publisher are recounted by Strahan himself in his preface to the original edition:

"During many years of his life he (Johnson) observed certain days with a religious solemnity; on which, and other occasions, it was his custom to compose suitable Prayers and Meditations, committing them to writing for his own use, and, as he assured me, without any view to their publication. But being last summer on a visit to Oxford to the Reverend Dr. Adams, and that gentleman urging him repeatedly to engage in some work of this kind, he then first conceived a design to revise these pious effusions, and bequeath them, with enlargements, to the use and benefit of others.

"Infirmities, however, now growing fast upon him, he at length changed this design, and determined to give the Manuscripts, without revision, in charge to me, as I had long shared his intimacy and was at this time his daily attendant. Accordingly, one morning, on my visiting him by desire at an early hour, he put these papers into my hands, with instructions for committing them to the press, and with a promise to prepare a sketch of his own life to accompany them. But the performance of the promise also was prevented, partly by his hasty destruction of some private memoirs, which he afterwards lamented, and partly by that incurable sickness, which soon ended in his dissolution."

It has been questioned whether Johnson ever really intended that his papers, thus turned over to Strahan, should be given to the public just as they stood, without revision or emendation. Says George Birbeck Hill, the latest editor of Prayers and Meditations which are included in his Johnsonian Miscellanies:

"That he should have wished his friend to publish all that is included in these Prayers and Meditations almost passes belief. Most likely, when in the weakness of his last days, he placed these papers in his hands, he forgot how much they contained that was meant for no eyes but his own."

If Johnson himself had made the revision discussed by him with Dr. Adams, it indeed seems likely that he would have confined himself to those passages in his papers which were of the largest general interest. That is to say, he would have suppressed the purely personal aspect of his struggles with the weaknesses peculiar to his own mind and body, his indolence, his intemperance in eating and drinking, his intense depression and melancholy, as well as the details of his daily life, of his fasting between Good Friday and

Easter, his maladies and of his treatment of them, in all of which particulars he might well think that the public had no legitimate interest. What he would have retained would have been the more general reflections and meditations such as might have ministered to all those suffering from moods arising from causes similar to those operating in his own case, and particularly the prayers which, since he himself had found comfort and strength in them, he might well have thought likely to prove beneficial to others of an equally pious and devout cast of mind.

If such is the case, the present editor may feel that he is to a certain extent carrying out at this late day the probable intention of Johnson himself in thus bringing together, as he has done, the hundred prayers, approximately, scattered throughout Strahan's volume as it has been augmented by successive editors from various sources, from time to time, and in making of them a book of devotion rather than a mere human document, however interesting and important this latter may be. If he has narrowed down too much the scheme of his selection, in choosing the prayers only, his plea is that in doing so he has secured a unity not otherwise attainable and that as the prayers are the fine flower of the collection, he has at least chosen to present the very highest expression of Johnson's spiritual life. Moreover, since it is not wholly possible to escape from the biographical interest in the prayers, and since therefore they require some comment on the circumstances under which they were composed, notes have been provided in which are given extracts from the more personal material in the Prayers and Meditations.

How fine the prayers themselves are, what a noble temple of religious devotion we have in this body of pious exhortations, needs no emphasis. The collection as a whole stands second to nothing of the kind in English literature, save the Book of Common Prayer of the Church of England, the outgrowth of many ages and many men's minds, whereas the prayers of Johnson are the expression and aspiration of a single human being through the round of a single individual experience. There was a superstitious and fantastic side to the religious devotion of Johnson, a touch of methodism, almost of mysticism, coloring the high-church orthodoxy of his faith. But one is scarcely conscious of this in the prayers themselves, which are the best expression of a rational piety seeking of God not so much an arbitrary intervention in the affairs of men, as spiritual strength and assistance to support the trials which are the common lot of humanity, that he may turn them to the best uses.

William Aspenwall Bradley.

[Acknowledgment is made of the assistance derived from the work of former editors, especially from the notes of George Birbeck Hill, which contain, in addition to other valuable data, the readings in the Pembroke College MSS. of the Prayers and Meditations. Johnson's own spelling and punctuation have been preserved in every instance. W. A. B.]

The Portrait was the recent portrait of Johnson painted by Sir Joshua Reynolds.

I. Introductory

INTRODUCTORY PRAYER   March 25, 1756.
This prayer designed by Johnson to be used as an introduction to any other prayer he might repeat, seems a most appropriate petition with which to preface the present collection as a whole.

II. Prayers composed by Dr. Johnson on New Year's Day

I.   January 1, $174\frac{4}{5}$.
From the final phrases in this prayer, it is evident that at the time of writing Johnson did not believe in the doctrine of purgatory or a middle state in which the souls of the dead could be benefited by the prayers of the living. Several years later, however (March 28, 1753), on the anniversary of the death of his wife, who had died in the preceding year, he wrote in his diary as follows: "In the evening I prayed for her conditionally, if it were lawful," showing that though he still harbored a doubt on this point, he had wavered in his conviction. So far as the Church of England is concerned, Johnson, who was a good churchman, was free to follow his own convictions in the matter, since it has never specifically defined its own position on the doctrine of purgatory, commending the practice of praying for the dead "as a very good and charitable deed," but refusing to guarantee its efficacy beyond counselling a trust in God "that he accepteth our prayers for them." It is easy to conceive, in seeking to account for Johnson's partial change of opinion, that the force of affliction and the intensity of his desire may well have softened his acceptance of an uncompromising theological dogma to the desire, at least, for a form of belief more sympathetic and consolatory to his bereavement.

II.   January 1, $174\frac{7}{8}$.

III.   January 1, $17\frac{49}{50}$, after three in the morning.
For "recollect," "improve" is scored out in the MS., and for "preservation," "support and comfort," likewise.

IV. January 1, 1753, N. S., which I shall use for the future. N. S., novum stylum, a new style of reckoning the date according to the corrected calendar adopted September 3, 1752, a change involving a loss of eleven days.

V. January 1, 1756, Afternoon. Boswell's editor, Malone, quotes the following from a letter to Dr. Joseph Wharton in elucidation of this passage: "For my part I have not lately done much. I have been ill in the winter, and my eye has been inflamed." Johnson's trouble with his eyes was more or less chronic. His affliction of scrofula had affected one eye to the point that he had very little use of it, though it was never totally blind, as some have thought, in support of which see the prayer entitled "When my Eye was Restored to Use," in the last Section,—a temporary restoration, however, as shown in the note to that prayer.

VI. January 1, 1757, at two in the morning. The part of the prayer following "Thy Holy Word" was at first scored through in the MSS., but he afterwards decided to let it stand.

VII. January 1, (1776), after two in the morning.

VIII. January 1, 1767, ... mane scripsi., i. e., "I wrote this early in the morning." No reference to the late hours kept by Johnson is necessary. He was afflicted with insomnia and dreaded nothing so much as what was for him the mockery of retiring to rest. The nights that were not spent by him convivially or in prolonged converse with those whom he could prevail upon to sit with him into the small hours, were frequently passed by him in solitary meditation or in religious exercises. Of course on nights like New Year's, there was an additional reason for prolonging the hours of wakefulness.

IX. January 1, 1769. Subjoined to this prayer are the words "Safely brought me to the beginning of this year." These words refer to the third Collect at Morning Prayer in the book of Morning Prayer, which he "accommodated" by altering "day" into "year" and "us" into "me." It begins: "O Lord, our heavenly Father, Almighty and Everlasting God, who hast safely brought us to the beginning of another day." This shows the uses to which he put his own prayers. He did not necessarily use them exclusively, or in place of the prayer-book, but most often in connection with the Collects for the day, prescribed by the Church, "accommodated" frequently, as in the present instance, to fit his personal needs.

X. Prima mane (i. e. early in the morning), January 1, 1770. After the words "or misery depress me" he had written: "Let my remaining days be innocent and useful," but afterwards struck them out. This prayer affords a good example of the state of depression and apprehension under which Johnson almost constantly labored. He suffered from a lethargy and inertness of the body and a melancholy and apathy of the mind that prevented him for long periods from accomplishing any work, and that led him, for the dissipation of his dullness and misery, into those indulgences against the seductions of which he petitions in this prayer. The disorder of his mind, which was largely the result of his own morbid imaginings, kept him in constant terror of madness and imbecility, the things which in the vigor of his intellect he feared most of all in this world. This prayer is included in all editions of Johnson's complete works in a separate section entitled Prayers. Twelve others from the present collection also are included in it.

XI. January 1, 1772, two in the morning. During the past year, Johnson's health and spirits had been much improved, and a correspondingly greater degree of composure is reflected than in the previous prayers. Here he prays for "purity of mind and holiness of life," and to be strengthened in "good purposes and reasonable meditations." This is in evident conformity with a fixed purpose to raise himself from the physical and mental slough into which he had fallen, by fixing his mind upon his spiritual duties. Johnson laid down many rules of conduct to this same end, and to this prayer he appends the oft-repeated resolution "to rise in the morning." Lying abed in the morning he considered to be his besetting sin. In 1753 he wrote: "I do not remember that since I left Oxford I ever rose early by mere choice, but once or twice at Edial, and two or three times for the Rambler."

XII. 1773, January 1, mane 1, 33, i. e., twenty-three minutes past one o'clock in the morning.

XIII.   1774, January 1, near two in the morning.
Johnson wrote of the past year: "This year has passed with so little improvement, that I doubt whether I have not rather impaired than increased my learning." "And yet," says Boswell, commenting on this passage in Prayers and Meditations, and referring to his own record of the year 1773, with its brilliant conversation, in which Johnson has conspicuously shone, "we have seen how he read, and we know how he talked during that period." Boswell was probably right in saying that the charges brought by Johnson against himself of idleness and lack of self-improvement through reading must be taken relatively and in view of what he himself felt that he was capable, with steady application, of performing.

XIV.   January 1, 1776.

XV.   Two p. m., January 1, 1777.
Followed by the first words of the Lord's Prayer, "Our Father." This is one of thirteen prayers included in the Complete **Works of Dr. Johnson**.

XVI.   January 1, 1779, before one in the morning.

XVII. 1780, January 1, h. 1 a.m., i. e. hora prima ante meridiem, or one o'clock at night.

XVIII.   1781 (January 2).
On this date Johnson writes: "I was yesterday hindered by my old disease of the mind and therefore begin to-day," explaining the lateness by one day of the last New Year's prayer which he wrote.

III. Prayers composed by Dr. Johnson on Easter Day

Easter was one of the most important occasions which Johnson reserved for special prayer and meditation. He approached the mystery of the Lord's Supper with a deep sense of its significance and holiness, and he prepared for it with curious rigor in the matter of fasting, any inadvertent violation of which caused him uneasiness, even anguish of mind. He records from Good Friday: "I had nothing but water once in the morning and once at bed-time. I refused tea after some deliberation." At another: "I fasted, though less rigourously than at other times. I by negligence poured milk into the tea, and, in the afternoon, drank one dish of coffee with Thrale." His regular observance of Easter began with the death of his wife, but of this we will speak more fully in a following note.

I. PRAYER ON EASTER DAY   April 22, 1753.
To whom, etc. : To whom be all honour and glory.
After this prayer, Johnson wrote, evidently at a later date: "This I repeated sometimes in church."

II.   Easter Eve, 1757.

III.   Easter Day, March 26, 1758.

IV.   Easter Day, April 15, 1759.
G. B. Hill writes that Johnson in his Dictionary does not give such a construction as "grant me chaste." Its condensation is in contrast with his characteristically expanded style. Indeed the prayers throughout are remarkable for their simplicity and directness of expression.
In this prayer Johnson prays for his father, his brother, his wife and his mother. The last mentioned had died this year. His father, Michael Johnson, had died in 1731. His brother, Nathanael, born in 1712, had died in 1737. There are no separate petitions for them in Prayers and Meditations, as Johnson had not begun to compose prayers at those dates.

V.   Easter Eve, 1761.
Preceding the prayer he writes down: "Since the Communion of last Easter I have led a life so dissipated and useless, and my terrors and perplexities have so much increased, that I am under great depression and discouragement, yet I purpose to present myself before God again tomorrow with humble hope that he will not break the promised word, Come unto me all ye that travail.

"I have resolved, I hope not presumptuously, till I am afraid to resolve again. Yet hoping in God I steadfastly propose to lead a new life. O God, enable me, for Jesus Christ's sake."
Then he resolves:
" To avoid idleness.
To regulate my sleep as to length and choice of hours.
To set down every day what shall be done the day following.
To keep a journal.
To worship God more diligently.
To go to church every Sunday.

To study the Scriptures.
To read a certain portion every week."
These resolutions are characteristic of those made on many other similar occasions, which seemed, however, never to be kept to his own satisfaction, as he reviews each year in retrospect.

VI. (1764.)

From the references in this prayer it is evident that it was written at a time of partaking communion, probably Easter. But it is not the regular Easter prayer for that year, which follows next in order in the present collection. It seems to have been inserted here conjecturally by the original editor, since the date is in brackets. Or it may be that the present prayer commemorates one of the two or three instances when Johnson received the sacrament on an other day than Easter Sunday. Fifteen years later, on September 18, 1779, he wrote: "My purpose is to communicate at least thrice a year," which purpose he repeats two years later, though rather as a hope than as a resolution. At this time, however, in 1764, he had formed no such resolution, merely recollecting to receive the sacrament every Easter Sunday. This was a pious duty enjoined upon him by the memory of his wife. On September 18, 1781, in adding a memorandum to the entry of Monday, April 16, of that year, he thanks God for having received "every year at Easter since the death of my poor dear Tetty." "I once," he says, "felt some temptation to omit it, but I was preserved from compliance. This was the thirtieth Easter."

VII. Easter Day, April 22, 1764, at 3 m.

On Good Friday this year Johnson wrote: "I have made no reformation, and have lived totally useless, more sensual in thought and more addicted to wine and meat." And on the following day he added: "A kind of strange oblivion has overpowered me, so that I know not what has become of the last year, and perceive that incidents and intelligence pass over me without leaving any impression. This is not the life to which Heaven is promised." Boswell attributes the increased indolence out of which this distress came in part to the independence attained through the royal pension granted him this year.

VIII.   Easter Day, April 7, 1765, about three in the morning.
"Oh God, have mercy on me."
IX.
This prayer was written the day before Easter, Saturday, March 29, 1766. He wrote at the same time: "I do not feel myself today so much impressed with awe of the approaching mystery. I had this day a doubt, like Baxter, of my state, and find that my faith, though weak, was yet faith. O God! Strengthen it." He expresses greater satisfaction with himself in the observation of his resolutions than is usual and notes that "since last New Year's Eve I have risen every morning by eight, at least not after nine, which is more superiority over my habits than I have ever before been able to obtain." The scruple about his faith, however, worries him, and it is against this form of morbid self-examination that he prays when in the present prayer he petitions that he "may no longer be distracted by doubts."
X.   Easter Day, March 15 (1770), in the morning.
XI.   Easter Day, March 31,—'71.
XII.   Easter Day, after twelve at night.
In another version of this prayer he thus varies the words to eject, etc., "to eject all wicked thoughts, to break off all sinful habits, and so to regulate my life that," &c.
XIII.   Nine in the morning.
This was the same day as the preceding. On March 15 of this year he wrote to Boswell: "My health grows better, yet I am not fully recovered. I believe it is held that men do not recover very fast after threescore."
XIV.   April 10, near midnight.
Written Saturday night, and used five times the following day as noted in his journal, both in church and in his private devotions.
XV.   Easter Day, April 16, 12.3, i.e. three minutes after twelve o'clock at night.
After this prayer Johnson has written: "Transcribed from a former book with a slight emendation or two. With that book I parted unnecessarily by a Catch." G. B. Hill hazards the opinion that by a catch he meant some sudden impulse or some scruple.

XVI.   1776, April 7, Easter Day.
"The time is again at which, since the death of my poor dear Tetty, on whom God have mercy, I have annually commemorated the mystery of the Redemption, and annually proposed to amend my life. My reigning sin, to which perhaps many others are appendant, is waste of time, and general sluggishness, to which I am always inclined, and in part of my life have been almost compelled by morbid melancholy and disturbance of mind. Melancholy has had in me its paroxysms and remissions, but I have not improved the intervals, nor sufficiently resisted my natural inclinations, or sickly habits. I will resolve henceforth to rise at eight in the morning, so far as resolution is hope, and will hope that God will strengthen me. I have begun this morning."

                                                                                                May 21.
"These resolutions I have not practiced nor recollected. O God grant me to begin now for Jesus Christ's sake. Amen."

XVII.   9nâ mane (nine o'clock in the morning).
Boswell quotes this and calls it an "emphatick prayer."

XVIII.   April 19, Easter Day, after twelve at night.

XIX. EASTER DAY PRAYER.   1779 (April 4).
It was Johnson's custom to endeavour, after having copied out his prayer and read it once or twice, to repeat it to himself, from memory, in church. On this occasion he notes, with the minute particularity that characterizes his journal, that he left out a clause.

XX.   Easter Eve, April 14, 1781.

XXI.   Easter Day, April 11, 1784.
This was the last Easter of Johnson's life, for he died on December 13 of the same year. He had been very ill in the winter, both of an asthma and of a dropsy. It was for his recovery from these diseases that he returns thanks in his prayer. He had, however, not so far regained his strength as to be permitted by his physicians to go to church, so the sacrament was administered to him at his own home. Of the sense of God's wrath, experienced by him before the danger of impending death, to which he refers in his prayer, he makes several allusions in his letters. To Mrs. Lucy Porter he wrote: "Death,

my dear, is very dreadful." And to Mrs. Thrale: "Write to me no more about dying with a grace; when you feel what I have felt in approaching eternity in fear of soon hearing the sentence of which there is no revocation, you will know the folly: my wish is, that you will know it sooner. The distance between the grave and the remotest point of human longevity is but a very little; and of that little no path is certain. You know all this, and I thought that I knew it too: but I know it now with a new conviction. May that conviction not be thine."

IV. Prayers composed by Dr. Johnson in memory of his wife.

In 1736, Johnson, at the age of twenty-seven, married Mrs. Elizabeth Porter, the widow of a clothier, and a woman twenty-one years older than himself. Despite the disparity of their ages, and all that has been said of Mrs. Johnson's lack of personal charms, to which indeed Johnson was quite blind, the marriage was a very happy one, and the death of his "Tetty" plunged him into a grief from which he never completely recovered. His sorrow often took on the form of self-reproach for his shortcomings towards her, but most frequently he tried to make her loss and the memory of her which he cherished strengthen him in his resolutions and lead him into higher ways of living. Two points connected with his devotions inspired by her we have mentioned in preceding notes: the conditional character of the prayers for her salvation, and the fact that it was at the time of her death that he took the resolution of celebrating communion regularly upon Easter Day. She died on March 17, o. s., or March 28, n. s., 1752.

I.   April 24, 1752.

II.   April 25, 1752.

We have no record of what these resolutions were that he made "on Tetty's coffin" as he refers to them in another passage.

III.   April 26, 1752, being after twelve at Night of the 25th. Johnson evidently had some sort of belief in the ability of the spirits of the dead to communicate with the souls of the living. How far this belief was justified in the present instance we do not know, as no reference was ever made by him to an apparition of his wife or any communication with her. He always had a deep-seated interest in so-called supernatural phenomena, to the proof or disproof of which he applied the laws of evidence much as he applied them to the support of the truth of the Bible story of the life of Christ and of the miracles contained in that narrative. He had no blind prejudice against admitting the possibility of events happening at variance with recognized laws of nature. In fact he was very far from conceiving anything like natural law as it is at present maintained by modern science. For him the human faculties of perception were the only evidence of truth or falsehood, and he was very fond of showing by ingenious examples how, in refusing to accept the testimony of our senses, in one instance, we must refuse to accept it in all, and that thus there would be nothing in the world as to the truth of which we could assume a practical assurance. Johnson was not superstitious. On the contrary he was in the highest degree rational in his treatment of the matter, however much this treatment may be at variance with that which prevails at the present day.

IV.   May 6, 1752.
The last part of the prayer follows Philippians, iv. 8: "Finally, brethren, whatsoever things are true, whatsoever things are honest, whatsoever things are just, whatsoever things are pure, whatsoever things are lovely, whatsover things are of good report; if there be any virtue and if there be any praise, think on these things!"

I.-V. These four prayers are grouped together by Johnson under this heading: "Prayers composed by me on the death of my wife, and reprinted among her memorials, May 8, 1752. Deus, exaudi. — Heu!"

May 6. I used this service, written April 24, 25, May 6, as preparatory to my return to life to-morrow.

V.   Fl. Lacr., March 28, in the Morning.
Fl. Lacr. is an abbreviation for flentibus lacrymis, or "with flowing tears."
This was in 1753, the first anniversary of the death of his wife. He wrote: "The melancholy of this day hung long upon me."

VI.   March 28, 1754, at Night.
He at first wrote: "Almighty God, by whose grace I have this day endeavoured," as an opening to this prayer.
VII.   March 28, '56, about two in the morning.
At first he wrote: "That however solitary," instead of "homes bereft of worldly comforts."
VIII.   March 28, 1758.
He had at first written: "Make me to enjoy the time for which thou shalt," etc., instead of the opening exordium as it now stands.
IX.   March 28, 1762.

V. Prayer composed by Dr. Johnson on his Birthday.

Johnson was born at Lichfield, in Staffordshire, on the 18th of September, N. S. 1709. His father, Michael Johnson, a bookseller, and his mother, Sarah Ford, were respectable people of the yeoman class. After attending several schools, he went to Oxford in 1728, and was entered as a Gentleman Commoner of Pembroke College. Johnson stayed at Oxford three years and then left without a degree. In 1732 he accepted a position as usher in a school in Market Bosworth. He also began to engage in literary work of an humble and obscure nature. In 1736 he married, as we have seen, and the same year he set up a private academy at Edial, near his native place. His venture, however, was not a success, and in 1737 he went up to London, bent upon supporting himself by writing for the publishers. The period covered by the Prayers and Meditations commences with 1729. A short chronology of the events of Johnson's life from the time of his coming to London is appended to the present volume.

I. A PRAYER ON MY BIRTHDAY.   September 7, 1738.
"This is the first solemn prayer of which I have a copy. Whether I composed any before this, I question."
A brief prayer is, however, included in the Prayers and Meditations under entry of September 7, 1736. He writes: "I have this day entered upon my 28th year. Mayest thou, O God, enable me for Jesus Christ's sake to spend this in such a manner that I may receive comfort from it at the hour of death and in the day of judgment. Amen."

II.   September 18, 1757.

III.   September 18, 1758, horâ primâ matutinâ, i. e. at one o'clock in the morning.

Instead of "the business of my station in this world" he had at first written: "The duties which thou shalt assign me, and to the duties by which"; and instead of "happy," in the last sentence, he had at first written "useful."

IV.   September 18, 1760, resolved D. j., i. e. Deo juvante, or God pleasing. Then follows a list of resolutions, preceding the prayer itself.

V.   September 7, 1764.

On the margin he wrote "18th," in correction of the date, which is according to old style.

VI.   September 18, 1776, at Streatham.

Streatham was the country place of the Thrales, to whose circle of acquaintance he had been admitted the year before. Thrale was a wealthy brewer, for whose character as a man of principle and of understanding Johnson had the highest esteem. It was Mrs. Thrale, however, in whom Johnson's interest in the family very largely centred. She was clever and attractive and vivacious, and Johnson maintained a sentimental friendship with her practically up to the time of his death.

VII.   September 18, 1768, at night. Townmalling in Kent. Townmalling was the country place of a Mr. Francis Brooke which Johnson mentions as one of "his favorite places."

VIII.   September 18, 1769.

"This day completes the sixtieth year of my age. What I have done and what I have left undone the unsettled state of my mind makes all endeavours to think improper. I hope to survey my life with more tranquillity, in some part of the time which God shall grant me.

"The last year had been wholly spent in a slow process of recovery. My days are easier, but the perturbation of my nights is very distressful. I think to try a lower diet. I have grown fat too fast. My lungs seem incumbered, and my breath fails me, if my strength is in any unusual degree exerted or my motions accelerated. I seem to myself to bear exercise with more difficulty than in the last winter. But though I feel all these decays of body I have made no preparation for the grave. What shall I do to be saved?"

September 18.

"Yesterday, having arisen from a disturbed and wearisome night, I was not much at rest the whole day. I prayed with the Collect, 'To the beginning,' in the night and in the morning. At night I composed my prayer and wrote my reflection. Reviewing them I found them both weakly conceived and imperfectly expressed, and corrected the prayer this morning. I am glad that I have not omitted my annual practice. I hope that by rigid temperance and moderate exercise I may yet recover. I used the prayer again at night, and am now to begin, by the permission of God, my sixty first year."

IX.   1771, September 18, 9 at night.

X.   Talisker in Skie, Sept. 24, 1773.

Johnson was at this time with Boswell on their tour of Scotland and the Hebrides.

"On last Saturday was my sixty-fourth birthday. I might perhaps have forgotten it had not Boswel told me of it." He speaks as if he would gladly have forgotten it, which is not unnatural, in view of the terrible crises through which he seemed to pass on each of the recurring anniversaries of his birth. He wrote to Mrs. Thrale at this time: "The return of my birthday, if I remember it, fills me with thoughts which it seems to be the general care of humanity to escape."

XI.   September 18, 1775.

"Composed at Calais in a sleepless night, and before the morn at Notre Dame written at St. Omers." His journey to France, which occupied about two months of this year, was undertaken in company with the Thrales.

XII.   Sept. 18, 1777, Ashbourn.

Ashbourn was the home of Dr. Taylor, a clerical friend of Johnson's, near Oxford, to which he often repaired.

XIII.   September 18, 1779, h. p. m., 12 ma., i. e. hora prima matutina, in the first hour in the morning, at twelve o'clock.

XIV.   September 18, 1780.

XV.   September 18, Vesp. 10° 40′ circ., i. e. about 10.40 o'clock at night.

"This is my seventy third birth-day — an awful day.... As I

came home [from church] I thought I had never begun any period of life so placidly."

Johnson gave a dinner on this birthday and invited two friends, Allen, his landlord, and Robert Levet, a bookseller. "I have always (been) accustomed to let this day pass unnoticed, but it came this time into my mind that some little festivity was not improper." Unnoticed, that is by any public or semi-public celebration of it.

XVI.   Ashbourn, September 18, 1784.
This prayer is not in the Pembroke MS., but was added by G. B. Hill from an original discovered by him in a private collection.

VI. Prayers composed by Dr. Johnson on several occasions.

I. Prayer on the "Rambler."
The "Rambler" was a semi-weekly paper started by Johnson in March 20, 1750, and continued by him almost single-handed for two years. The papers were afterwards collected, the work running through ten editions in his lifetime. This prayer is quoted by Boswell in his Life.

II. Before any new study.   November (1752).

III. After Time negligently and unprofitably spent.
                                            November 19 (1752).

IV.   Apr. 3, 1753.
This prayer is quoted in the Life. It is preceded by the following entry: "I began the second vol. of my Dictionary, room being left in the first for Preface, Grammar and History, none of them yet begun." The dictionary to which specific reference is made in this prayer was begun in 1747 and finished in 1755. He expected to do it in three years. At the time of this prayer, therefore, three years after the time allotted had expired, he had completed only about one half the work.

V. On the Study of Philosophy as an Instrument of Living.
                                                     July (1754).
Boswell refers to this prayer in the Life: "In July this year," says Boswell, "he (Johnson) had formed some scheme of mental improvement, the particular purpose of which does not appear." The particular significance of the prayer is that

Johnson now having finished his Dictionary, he was casting about for a new employment. After the prayer he wrote later: "This study was not persued."

VI. Hill Boothby's Death.   January 1786.

This prayer, like the one before it, is not in the Pembroke MSS. Hill Boothby was one of the many women for whom Johnson entertained a sentimental affection. In fact he grew intensely jealous of her preference for Lord Lyttleton and at one time conceived an animosity toward her on that account. She died at the age of forty-seven, and Mme. Piozzi (Mrs. Thrale) says: "I have heard Baretti say, that when the lady died, Dr. Johnson was almost distracted with his grief; and that the friends about him had much ado to calm the violence of his emotion."

VII. When my Eye was restored to its Use.
                                                February 15, 1756.

Four days later he wrote: "The inflammation is again come into my eye."

This prayer is not in the Pembroke College MSS., but is quoted in the Life.

VIII.   Jan. 23, 1759.

Johnson's mother died in Lichfield at the age of ninety. Johnson had not seen her for several years, and tried in vain to reach her during her last illness. To defray the expenses of her funeral, he wrote "Rasselas," for which he received one hundred pounds.

Johnson's letters to his mother and to his step-daughter, Lucy Porter, who was in attendance on her when he heard of her condition, are very affecting. One reads as follows:

"Dear honored mother:

"Neither your condition nor your character make it fit for me to say much. You have been the best mother, and I believe the best woman in the world. I thank you for your indulgence to me, and beg forgiveness of all that I have done ill, and all that I have omitted to do well. God grant you his Holy Spirit, and receive you to everlasting happiness, for Jesus Christ's sake. Amen. Lord Jesus receive your spirit. Amen.

"I am, dear, dear Mother,
              "Your dutiful son,
                        "Sam. Johnson."

Preceding the prayer are these words: "The day on which my dear mother was buried. Repeated on my fast, with the addition." The addition, really a separate prayer, reads as follows:

"And, O Lord, grant unto me that am now about to return to the common comforts and business of the world, such moderation in all enjoyments, such diligence in honest labour, and such purity of mind, that, amidst the changes, miseries, or pleasures of life, I may keep my mind fixed upon thee, and improve every day in grace, till I shall be received into thy kingdom of eternal happiness." [Amen.]

The fast referred to was held on March 24, the date of the prayer next in order.

IX. March the 24, 1759, rather 25, after 12 at night, jej., i.e. jejinus, fasting.

Concerning the change of outward things referred to, Boswell writes: "What particular new scheme of life Johnson had in view this year I have not discovered, but that he meditated one of some sort is clear from his private devotions.... But he did not, in fact, make any external or visible change." He however had moved the day before from his house in Gough Square to lodgings in Staple Inn, and it is this, no doubt, to which he had reference.

X. Before the Study of Law.   Sept. 26, 1765.

"He appears this year to have been seized with a temporary fit of ambition, for he had thought both of studying law and of engaging in politicks." Boswell.

XI. Engaging in Politicks with H—n.   Nov. 1765.

H—n: the Right Honourable William Gerard Hamilton.

In the preceding note Boswell was quoted to the effect that Johnson entertained the ambition of entering into politics. Strahan corrects him on this point and says that Johnson had no intention of himself entering upon a political career with Hamilton, but merely meant to furnish his friend with "his sentiments on the great political topics which should be considered in parliament." The effort was once made to have Johnson enter parliament, but nothing came of it.

XII.   March 7, 1766.

Entering N. M. (Novum Museum) i.e. new study. Johnson had

moved from Staple Inn into a house in Johnson's Court, Fleet Street, the year previous.

XIII. August 17, 1767.
It was at this time that Johnson began to abstain from the use of wine and suppers, from which he says he "obtained sudden and great relief."
Following this prayer are a list of collects employed with it:
O God who desirest not the Death, &c.,
O Lord grant us encrease—
O God,— pardon and peace,
O God who knowest our necessities,
Our Father.
"He has apparently in mind the Absolutions and the Collects from the fourteenth and twenty-first Sundays after Trinity and the last Collect but one in the Communion Service in the Book of Common Prayer." G. B. Hill.

XIV. Oct. 18, 1767, Sunday.
"Yesterday, Oct. 17, at about ten in the morning, I took my leave forever of my dear old friend Catherine Chambers, who came to live with my mother about 1724, and has been but little parted from us since. She buried my Father, my Brother and my Mother. She is now fifty-eight years old.
"I desired all to withdraw, then told her that we were to part for ever, that as Christians we should part with prayer, and that I would, if she was willing, say a short prayer beside her. She expressed great desire to hear me, held up her poor hands, as she lay in bed, with great fervour, while I prayed kneeling by her, nearly in the following words: [The prayer follows.]
"I then kissed her. She told me that to part was the greatest pain that she had ever felt, and that she hoped we should meet again in a better place. I expressed with swelled eyes and great emotion of tenderness the same hope. We kissed and parted. I humbly hope, to meet again, and part no more."
This is quoted in the Life.

XV. Bed-time. Lent 2 (1768).
"The following prayer, which is not in the Pembroke College MSS., is an 'accommodation' of the Collect for the Second Sunday in Lent." G. B. Hill.
"This prayer may be said before or after the entrance into bed, as a preparative for sleep."

"When I transcribed this Prayer, it was my purpose to have made this book a Collection." The book referred to here was a parchment book known to Strahan. Many of the other prayers are marked "Transcribed" under this same date.

XVI. Scruples.
"Of this prayer there is no date, nor can I conjecture when it was composed." Probably composed before 1766, as there is a reference to it in the entry of that date.

XVII. Study of Tongues.
"Of this Prayer there is no date, nor can I tell when it was written; but I think it was in Gough-square, after the Dictionary was ended. I did not study what I have intended." This prayer is not in the Pembroke MSS.

XVIII.   November 5, 1769.
"This I found Jan. 11, —72; and believe it written when I began to live on milk. I grew worse with forbearance of solid food."

XIX.   July 25, 1776.
"When I purposed to apply vigorously to study particularly of the Greek and Italian tongues.
"Repeated July 3, —77 about 12 at night."

XX. Thanksgiving.   Sunday, June 18, 1780.
"In the morning of this day last year I perceived the remission of those convulsions in my breast which had distressed me for more than twenty years. I returned thanks at Church for the mercy granted me, which has now continued a year."

XXI.   1781, June 22.
Henry Thrale had died on Wednesday, April 4, and had been buried on the 11th.
"I felt about the last flutter of his pulse, and looked for the last time upon the face that for fifteen years had never been turned upon me but with respect and benignity. Farewell. May God that delighteth in mercy, have had mercy on thee."

XXII. At the table.

XXIII. At departure or at home.
"These prayers I wrote for Mrs. Lucy Porter in the latter end of the year 1782, and transcribed them October 9, —84." John-

son was staying at the home of his step-daughter at the time of the transcription.

XXIV. (On leaving Streatham).   October 6, 1782.
Concerning this departure, Boswell wrote: "The death of Mr. Thrale had made a very material alteration with respect to Johnson's reception in that family. The manly authority of the husband no longer controlled the lively exuberance of the lady: and as her vanity had been fully gratified, by having the Colossus of Literature attached to her for many years, she gradually became less assiduous to please him."
Boswell quotes this prayer with the remark: "One cannot read this prayer without some emotions not very favourable to the lady whose conduct occasioned it."
The next day Johnson wrote:
"I was called early. I packed up my bundles, and used the foregoing prayer, with my morning devotions somewhat, I think, enlarged. Being earlier than the family I read St. Pauls farewell in the Acts, and then read fortuitously in the Gospels, which was my parting use of the library."

XXV.   July 30.
"G. Strahan inserts this prayer among those of which it is not known in what year they were written. It belongs to 1783, at a time when Johnson had recovered from the stroke of palsy, and was troubled with a complaint which threatened him with a surgical operation." G. B. Hill.

XXVI. Prayer for Mrs. Williams during her illness preceding her death in 1783.   (August, 1783).
Mrs. Williams was a lady who had long lived on Johnson's bounty, one of his many pensioners.
"From the fly-leaf of a copy of the fifth edition of Prayers and Meditations (1817) in the possession of Mr. C. E. Doble. There is nothing to show who transcribed the prayer or whence it was taken. The title is not Johnson's, for it begins 'Prayer of Dr. Johnson.' Moreover it is not correct, for though the prayer is partly for her it is still more for him." G. B. Hill.

XXVII.   September 6.
"I had just heard of Williams' death."
This prayer is not in the Pembroke College MSS.

XXVIII.   August 1, 1784, Ashbourne.
Not in the Pembroke MSS. The original was found by G. B. Hill in a private collection.

XXIX. Against inquisitive and perplexing thoughts.
                                          Aug. 12, —84.
Quoted in the Life. This prayer is very characteristic of the way Johnson met the ultimate mysteries of existence. It was the way he kept his underlying pessimism from destroying his religious faith as it did in the case of Voltaire.

XXX.   Aug. 28, 1784, Ashbourne.
Hill says that the blank must be filled with Taylor's name. Ashbourne was his place at which Johnson was staying.

XXXI. Prayer on the study of Religion.
One of the prayers to which no date can be assigned, as with the next three.

XXXII. The last six lines are quoted in the Life.

XXXIII. This prayer is not in the Pembroke College MSS.

XXXIV. This prayer is not in the Pembroke College MSS.

XXXV.
(The following prayer was composed and used by Doctor Johnson previous to receiving the Sacrament of the Lord's Supper, on Sunday, December 5, 1784. Note by G. Strahan.)
"This prayer is not in Johnson's handwriting." G. B. Hill.
Quoted in the Life.

"Rest Eternal," etc. "Accommodated" in Johnson's own manner from an old liturgy in use in the Anglican Church, as a fitting conclusion to the Prayers.

OF this book there have been printed at the McClure Press seven hundred and fifty copies in three editions, as follows: Five hundred copies on machine-made paper which are numbered from two hundred and fifty-one to seven hundred and fifty. Two hundred copies on English hand-made paper from the Kelmscott Mills which are numbered from fifty-one to two hundred and fifty; and fifty copies on Imperial Japan vellum which are numbered from one to fifty.

This is number

CPSIA information can be obtained at www.ICGtesting.com
Printed in the USA
LVOW04s1149271015

459943LV00001B/212/P